W9-DCF-857

THINKING ENGLISH CANADA

ALSO BY PHILIP RESNICK

The Land of Cain (1977)

Parliament vs. People (1984)

The Masks of Proteus: Canadian Reflections on the State (1990)

Letters to a Québécois Friend (1990)

Toward a Canada–Quebec Union (1991)

THINKING
ENGLISH
CANADA

PHILIP RESNICK

Published in 1994 by
Stoddart Publishing Co. Limited
34 Lesmill Road
Toronto, Canada
M3B 2T6
(416) 445-3333

Canadian Cataloguing in Publication Data

Resnick, Philip, 1944–
Thinking English Canada

ISBN 0-7737-2759-0

1. Canadians, English-speaking.*
2. Multiculturalism–Canada.*
I. Title.

FC141.R47 1994   971.064'7   C93-095523-4
F1035.B7R48 1994

Typesetting: Tony Gordon Ltd.
Printed and bound in Canada

*Stoddart Publishing gratefully acknowledges the support of the
Canada Council, Ontario Ministry of Culture, Tourism, and
Recreation, Ontario Arts Council, and Ontario Publishing Centre
in the development of writing and publishing in Canada.*

Contents

Acknowledgements

THIS BOOK OWES MUCH to the Canadian people who, by refusing to go along with their betters during the October 1992 referendum, ensured that issues of national identity and democratic empowerment would remain important ones to continue to address. The author also wishes to thank his colleague Alan Cairns, for useful comments, now as in the past; Don Blake, for help with computer programming; Petula Muller, for her secretarial prowess; Michael Davis of House of Anansi Press, and Don Bastian and Michael Carroll of Stoddart Publishing, for editorial assistance; and Mahie for, once again, putting up with *mes folies*.

Introduction: Enter the Bloc

CANADIANS HAVE RECENTLY BEEN through a federal election that resulted in a majority Liberal government and a Parliament unlike any we have known before. The Conservatives and the New Democratic Party (NDP) were both decimated, with the Reform Party emerging as a new voice of protest on the right in English Canada. But it is the presence of a sizable group of Bloc Québécois (BQ) MPs — 54 of the 75 from Quebec — that merits our attention. Not only does the Bloc enjoy the position of Official Opposition in Ottawa; it brings directly into the federal arena the concerns of a Quebec nationalist movement that has been gathering steam ever since the Quiet Revolution of the 1960s.

Much like the initial election of René Lévesque and the Parti Québécois (PQ) in Quebec on November 15, 1976, the success of the Bloc Québécois on October 25, 1993, should bring home to the rest of Canada the degree to which a majority of francophone Québécois feel themselves alienated from Canada as we know it. Lucien Bouchard and the Bloc promise to do to federal politics what Charles Parnell and the Irish Nationalists did in the late 19th century, by placing the issue of home rule for Ireland front and centre in British politics.

Fatigued as most of us may have been by the intensive constitutional debate from the Meech Lake Accord of 1987 to the Charlottetown Accord of 1992, we need to brace ourselves for a whole new round of discussions. True, much will depend on the outcome of the provincial election in Quebec in 1994 and on a subsequent referendum on sovereignty, should the Parti Québécois form the next

Quebec government. But the Bloc Québécois's capture of about half the popular vote in Quebec in the 1993 federal election suggests that we in English Canada need to begin to prepare ourselves for a fundamental restructuring of our federation.

I originally set out to write this book in the aftermath of the failed referendum of October 26, 1992, for I was convinced then, and remain even more convinced today, that the federal arrangements Canada has known since 1867 are doomed. A one-nation Canada — the same for English-speaking Canadians, Québécois, and aboriginal peoples — is of yesterday, not tomorrow. Few in francophone Quebec or among our aboriginal population still subscribe to it. It is we, the largely English-speaking population of the rest of Canada, who have to get on with the challenging task of rethinking our identity and national institutions.

The debate about Charlottetown, as such, is now history, and I have accordingly consigned my discussion of it to an appendix. But in an era that has seen three multinational federations — Yugoslavia, the Soviet Union, and Czechoslovakia — bite the dust in rapid succession, one would be foolish in the extreme to assume that Canada is invulnerable. We may well be next in line for the mapmakers, as the surge of support for the Bloc Québécois would suggest.

Still, the future is open-ended. It is not inevitable that Canada will splinter into two or more nation-states. What is inevitable, however, is that English-speaking Canadians must begin to grapple with their identity without illusions. To the degree that a majority of Québécois have been defining themselves as *Québécois d'abord* — Quebeckers first — it follows that they are consciously placing the putatively Canadian pole of their identity a distinct second. This fact is no less true for many self-proclaimed federalists in Quebec as for overt Quebec sovereigntists. We must stop imagining that we, who see ourselves as Canadians first, can share a single concept of nation with them. In similar fashion, the logic of aboriginal demands presses against an exclusively Canadian pole of identity in favour of something different — the acknowledgement of primordial forms of identity predating the European colonization of this country. While the exact political forms that aboriginal identity may take remain to be determined and the geographical dispersion of aboriginal peoples contrasts with the relative concentration and cultural cohesion of francophone Quebeckers, these claims also challenge any monolithic conception of Canadian identity. In an important sense, English-speaking Canada is something other than Québécois or aboriginal. (That significant parts of the present territory of Quebec are themselves aboriginal further complicates the equation.)

Yet what exactly is English Canada? How does one come to terms with its far-flung geographical character, its regional loyalties, its multicultural dimensions? What are some of the ideological strains in English-Canadian political culture? What about our relationship to the larger English-speaking world of which we are a part, and with the single most important English-speaking power with which we share a continent, the United States? How well or poorly will we be able to pull ourselves together when faced with the sort of political challenges that Quebec's demands and those of our aboriginal people pose? These are some of the themes addressed in this book.

Some of my initial reflections take me beyond the Canadian case to an examination of the nation-state relationship elsewhere, and of the comparative experience of federal states of the multinational sort. The remainder of the discussion, while firmly rooted in Canada, is also unbounded by the conventional view, at least in English-speaking Canada, of nationality, citizenship, and state. For my point of departure is that we need to distinguish nationality from citizenship, and our identity as English-speaking Canadians from our membership in a larger political framework that includes Québécois and aboriginal peoples.

We need to start exploring the identity of English Canada — the place of language in its makeup, the nature of its culture, the very terminology we use to discuss it. How acceptable a term is *English Canada* to describe some 20 million people of diverse backgrounds and origins, living in the northern part of North America and using English as their lingua franca? Is English Canada a real geographical entity, one coloured by elements of shared geography and history, and by the identities of its composite regions? Is it better approached as a state of mind, something that appeals to the imagination and builds on bonds of community forged among its inhabitants? Or is it, as some might argue, nothing more than an entirely artificial construct that serves at best to describe what remains of Canada once Quebec and the aboriginal peoples have been symbolically hived off?

The purpose of what follows is not to offer hard and fast answers to questions of this sort. It is to try to spark a long-overdue discussion of an entity — English Canada — that, in important respects, refuses to speak its name. It is to at least pose the possibility of thinking of English Canada as a society with an identity of its own. For English Canada, as I see it, is more than a foil to the identities of others. It is potentially a nation in its own right, one with its own particular vision and place within the Canadian ensemble.

What is required at this point is not a programmatic statement of what English Canada ought to be. Rather, we need to advance discussion across traditional regional and party lines in the spirit of what occurred during some of the constitutional debates of 1991–1992. If we are to deal with the inevitable institutional restructuring that faces this country, we must, as English-speaking Canadians, begin a dialogue with one another as members of a single national community.

1

Nation and State

I N THE *Concise Oxford Dictionary*, we find the following definition of nation: "Large number of people of mainly common descent, language, history, etc., usually inhabiting a territory bounded by defined limits and forming a society under one government." And in *Micro Robert*, a leading French dictionary, one reads: "A quite vast human grouping, which is characterized by consciousness of its unity and by a will to live together" (my translation). Something of the Canadian predicament regarding nation is embodied in these two passages.

In the English-speaking world, there is a tendency to identify nation with government or state. We assume quite readily that the government of any particular country is the *national* government. We assume that the claim of a group to be a nation will automatically translate into the language of sovereign statehood. We think of nation-states as the primary units in international relations and have named the major world organization the United Nations. The possibility of disaggregating nation from state does not come easily or naturally.

There are good historical reasons why English speakers would view things so. In Great Britain, despite the separate historical experiences of England, Scotland, and Wales, the existence of a single state with common institutions — monarchical, parliamentary, legal — since the beginning of the 17th century has helped engender a shared sense of community. British economic ascendancy in the 18th and 19th centuries and the flourishing of an overseas empire further cemented a consciousness of nationality to which a single language and a largely Protestant religion also contributed significantly. (It is religion, after all, that proved the major obstacle to the permanent absorption of Ireland into the United Kingdom.)

The United States, in some ways, emulated the British experience. A common history of British colonization, of revolution and overthrow of British rule, led to the creation of a new political structure with the Constitution of 1787. The federal republic thus created played a signal role in engendering a new sense of national consciousness, something reinforced by the victory of the North in the American Civil War. American economic development and the country's rise to world power status in the 20th century made the issue of American nationality a relatively uncontested matter, even after millions of immigrants poured in from Europe and elsewhere. (As with the Irish in the United Kingdom, blacks in the United States remained for a long time an unassimilated, nay excluded, group from common citizenship.)

There has, therefore, been a significant overlapping of the notion of state with that of nation in the English-speaking world and a pattern where the first tends to generate the second, a phenomenon that has also partially been at work in other ex-British colonies, especially of the settler variety. Could one really argue that a Canadian, an Australian, or a New Zealander nationality existed before dominions with these names were created? Can one discuss national identities in these instances in isolation from common political structures and, therefore, citizenship?

It is when we leave the English-speaking world that we find ourselves up against an alternative pattern of thinking. A sense of nationality often precedes the creation of any common state structure. One thinks of the kingdoms and duchies of Germany or of Italy and of common threads of national feeling preceding state unity in 1870–71. One thinks of attempts to forge a sense of nationhood in the Czech, Hungarian, or South Slavic lands under Hapsburg rule. One thinks of the ebb and flow of national consciousness in areas such as the Baltic countries, the Ukraine, or the Caucasus under both tsars and commissars.

Even where nation and state came to be conjoined as in both France and Spain in early modern times, older loyalties persisted.

Bretons, Provençals, and Alsatians were not French speakers like Parisians; Basques and Catalans were not Castilians. Although centralizing monarchs attempted to impose a single rubric of administration, national feeling was not so easily inculcated. Instinctively, local populations and elites resisted the best-laid plans to force them into a single mould and to forget what made them different.

The coming of revolution and of the Napoleonic Wars brought novel forces into play, most importantly the principle of popular sovereignty. At one level, this served to homogenize national sentiments, as in the notion of the republic one and indivisible in France, or in resistance to French incursions into other European lands, for example, Spain, Prussia, and Russia. At another level, it served to underline the importance of national consciousness as something linked to, yet separate from, the state. The mobilization of newly enfranchised citizens helped lead the revolutionary and Napoleonic armies to their initial victories. Patriotism crossed familiar occupational, sectional, and regional lines; it was the harbinger of a style of politics where, unlike what had been the case in the dynastic and absolutist regimes of Europe, mass public opinion mattered.

I am not implying here that nationalism would necessarily take a revolutionary form. It could be harnessed to powerfully conservative, even counterrevolutionary ideas as in 19th-century Germany or Russia. It could link up with religion as in various parts of the Christian world, the Middle East and North Africa, and the Indian subcontinent. It could be more or less urban or rural, more or less tolerant or intolerant, more or less middle-class, more or less white or mestizo or indigenous, as the case might be.

Nationalism could also give rise to persistent rivalries between ethnic, religious, or linguistic groups, both within Europe and beyond its boundaries, as it spread to the New World, to Africa, or to Asia. One saw this process occur in wholesale fashion in Eastern and Central Europe in the aftermath of World War I. What were the historical boundaries of Poland, and what about the significant Ukrainian, German, Lithuanian, and Jewish minorities within the newly created state? Would they be Poles in the same way as the ethnic and religious majority? What about the Sudeten Germans or the Hungarians in Czechoslovakia, or what about the cohesion between Czechs and Slovaks? What about the ethnic minorities of Hungary, Romania, and the different regions of Yugoslavia, Bulgaria, or Greece?

The potentially explosive character of ethnic nationalism was evident enough in the mass extermination of Armenians or the expulsion of Greeks by Turkey; in the Nazi holocaust against Jews and Gypsies; in the wholesale displacement and suppression of national minorities in Stalinist Russia. Within the emerging nationalist movements of the colonial world, divisions were also rampant: Hindu versus Muslim in British India; Vietnamese versus non-Vietnamese in Indochina; dominant ethnic or religious group versus minority ones in Southeast Asia, the Arab world, East and West Africa; and so on.

In reality, the political borders of most states that have been created in the half century since World War II have coincided very imperfectly with national sentiment among their populations. Scores of nationalist movements, from Slovak to Slovenian, Zionist to Algerian, Bangladeshi to Indonesian, eventually succeeded in achieving the goal of nation-state status. Scores of others have not. The political map of Africa is an artificial reflection of the colonial divisions of a century before. For their part, tribal peoples in China, Burma, and Afghanistan, as well as Kurds, Palestinians (until recently), Berbers, and indigenous peoples in much of the New World, have had their identities denied.

Yet are they any less distinct peoples despite their political subordination to others? Are ethnic minorities in countries where historical rivalries run deep any less prone to national feeling than ethnic majorities? Can we even assume that long-unified states are invulnerable to forces of internal nationalism?

I am not about to argue that national sentiment and political statehood are unconnected, or that the approximately 200 sovereign states of the late 20th century are not privileged units within an international system whose roots go back to the Treaty of Westphalia. What is much more contestable, however, is the proposition that national sentiment and political statehood are one and the same — that all nations must constitute states and all states nations.

If we go back to the *Micro Robert* definition of nation cited at the beginning of this chapter, we see that it speaks about a human grouping with "consciousness of its unity" and with "a will to live together." This definition speaks less about political statehood and a good deal more about existential feeling. It addresses the sense of being a community that may be the outgrowth of a long historical span or of modernity itself, that may draw upon such features of commonality as language, culture, religion, or social organization. These may or may not be common to those who live within a particular set of political boundaries; for certain groups, they may well span such boundaries. The empires of the modern world, from the Austro-Hungarian, the Russian, or the Ottoman to the British or the French, contained within them multiple national groupings. So, too, do a large number of contemporary nation-states.

Two examples drawn from Western Europe can help illustrate this fact. Spain, for almost 500 years, from the time of those most Catholic of monarchs, Ferdinand and Isabella, to the rule of the dictator Francisco Franco, practised a policy of systematic centralization. Yet since the restoration of democracy in 1977, Catalonia, the Basque country, and Andalusia have acquired the status of autonomous regions. During the Barcelona Olympics of 1992, for example, the Catalan government went to exceptional lengths — advertisements in the international press, status for Catalan as one of the official Olympic languages, the singing of the Catalan and Spanish anthems at opening and closing ceremonies — to emphasize Catalonia's distinctiveness. In similar fashion, the Flemish and Walloon regions of Belgium have increasingly asserted their own identities and power at the expense of the Belgian state. Yet the de facto capital of the European Community and site of the European Commission is Brussels.

Even where economic integration has been the norm, therefore, we have seen the remarkable persistence or revival of cultural nationalism, something that is equally true within states such as Italy, France, or the United Kingdom, in the form of the Northern Leagues and Corsican and Scottish nationalism. We can also see such continuing nationalism in the relations of individual states to larger structures like the European Community; the hostility toward the

Maastricht Treaty in various European countries offers a case in point.

When we extend our horizons to the post-Communist states of Eastern Europe and the ex-Soviet Union, to the Middle East, the Indian subcontinent, and Africa in its many parts, we become even more aware of the poor fit between political statehood and national identities. The breakup of the Soviet Union, for example, has left in its wake a maze of ethnic minorities in each of the successor republics. It does not appear that majority ethnic groups willingly extend equal citizenship rights to minorities in a sizable number of these republics. In Yugoslavia, armed warfare and ethnic cleansing have provided nightly television reminders of the procrustean price of insisting that political boundaries coincide with ethnic or communal ones. Elsewhere, who outside official circles really believes that a single concept of citizenship organically binds Kurd to Iraqi or Turk, Punjabi Sikh to Kashmiri Muslim or Bihari Hindu, Ibo to Hausa in Nigeria, indigenous peoples to European-descended populations in much of the Americas? National sentiment is more than a matter of formal citizenship or identity cards.

At some deeper level, then, when we talk about nation in contradistinction from state, we are speaking about group affinity and shared values. The values in question may be cultural, linguistic, religious, or ethnic, but they tend to establish distinctions between a we-group and those outside it. Those distinctions may be hard and fast or flexible; they may be perfectly compatible with overlapping commitments, for example, to one's own group and some larger political one, or not, for instance, when there is no such openness to mutual coexistence and diversity.

There are far more national groupings in the world, using the above criteria, than there are nation-states, which is not to suggest that every ethnic, religious, or cultural grouping within a particular state has consciousness of itself as a "nation," or that we need extend this term to any community, small or large, that wishes to claim it. Historical factors, shared sentiment, ongoing viability, geographical and political space in which to live a common destiny may all need to be considered. And many national groupings will fall by the wayside, in the same way that history records the rise and fall of different linguistic and cultural communities, no less than political units, through the ages.

Still, why should we reserve the national label for sovereign states? Not only does this have a social Darwinian quality to it — only sovereign political actors really count in the world of realpolitik — but it places too much weight on purely political factors at the expense of social and cultural ones. So much of national sentiment has to do with day-to-day socialization and shared cultural identities. For many communities of people, it has little to do with the coercive and often alien activities of the state, military or civilian, and everything to do with what they can determine for themselves. The values they cherish may be thoroughly traditional or relatively modern, collectivist or individualist, but they speak to the ethos of their particular national grouping.

The more willing we are to embrace sociological diversity in our understanding of nationality, the greater the possibility of making progress in resolving conflicts that national differences engender. For once we abandon the fetish that state and nation are one and the same thing, we free ourselves from another idée fixe, namely that recognizing a people as a nation inexorably means recognizing the desirability of their forming a state. There are economic, political, demographic, and strategic considerations that inevitably enter into the establishment or recognition of new states; there can be rather different considerations involved where the status of nations is concerned.

Let us return to the Canadian context. As long as we operate under the assumption, as a majority of English Canadians does, that there is a single Canadian nation formed in 1867 of which Québécois and aboriginal peoples are a constituent part, there is relatively little room for discussion. We are involved in a zero-sum game in which the very survival of the political unit, Canada, whose citizenship we espouse, seems threatened by any concessions on the subject of nationhood.

In mirror-image fashion, those, be they Québécois or aboriginals, who associate nationhood with sovereignty leave little alternative to political confrontation or secessionist meltdown. How could a self-respecting national grouping settle for less, if the model of nation its adherents espouse is indeed the one advanced by the *Concise Oxford* definition cited earlier, namely, "a society under one government?" How could they possibly accept two or more levels of government, particularly when their national grouping can enjoy only permanent minority status within the more extensive of these?

Once we grant, however, that aboriginal nations or a Quebec nation are not the same thing as aboriginal nation-states or a sovereign Quebec, multiple possibilities come to mind. We can imagine a significant measure of autonomy for each of these within some ongoing Canadian ensemble. We can imagine overlapping loyalties between a specifically aboriginal or Québécois pole of identity and a Canada within which one's national distinctiveness is acknowledged. We can start envisaging constitutional arrangements — asymmetrical, confederal, or what have you — in which the aspirations of minority nationalities and of the English-Canadian majority are fully provided for.

Working out new institutional arrangements, as our recent experience with both Meech and Charlottetown suggests, is, of course, another matter. It is by no means certain that a majority of English Canadians — or for that matter even sizable numbers of Québécois and aboriginals — are quite ready for the difficult negotiations and inevitable trade-offs that would accompany reorganization of the Canadian state on the basis of multiple national identities. Still, to the degree that we can separate sociological nationhood from political statehood, we may be able to address an issue that has dogged other states around the world with significant linguistic, cultural, or ethnic minorities.

Nowhere has this problem been more acute than in states of a multinational variety, especially multinational federations. So let us turn to some of the difficulties these have been encountering in recent years, the better to see where the dialectic of state and nation may lead us.

2

The Crisis of Multinational Federations

IN DECEMBER 1991, the Union of Soviet Socialist Republics, proud offspring of the Bolshevik Revolution and superpower of the post-World War II period, disappeared. In its place rose some 15 independent republics, a number of incipient civil and interstate wars, and a paper Commonwealth of Independent States. That same year, as well, the Yugoslav federation ceased to exist. Slovenia achieved its independence peacefully enough, but Croatia and Serbia fought a murderous war, followed by an even bloodier three-way conflict in Bosnia-Herzegovina, which has seen that republic largely carved up between ethnic Serbs and Croats. Then, on January 1, 1993, the Federal Republic of Czechs and Slovaks became two separate states. Clearly the 1990s do not look very promising for multinational federations.

Before we look more closely at the fate that has befallen these three federations, and the possible fate that awaits others like our own, let us pause to ask a question. What exactly is a multinational federation and in what ways does it differ from other federations?

Canadians often compare themselves to Americans. We are usually conscious of some of the differences between our countries' systems — a parliamentary versus congressional; a distribution of powers in Canada originally weighted more toward the centre; the greater importance of rights and judicial interpretation thereof in the American as compared to the pre-charter Canadian system — but we are still both continent-wide federations. And whatever the peculiarities that the presence of Quebec brings to the Canadian case or slavery brought to the American South before the Civil War, it would seem that we share this feature.

Appearances, however, can be deceptive. Federations such as the United States, or for that matter Australia and Germany, do not have the same nature as federations such as Canada, Switzerland, India, or the ex-Soviet Union. The key distinction is that countries in the first group tend to have a single official language and thereby, despite important regional or ethnic diversity, a degree of cultural homogeneity across the different units. Countries in the second group have two or more official languages, which in turn introduces cultural heterogeneity into the very social fabric. We speak of French Canadians or English Canadians, French Swiss or German Swiss, Hindi-speaking or Tamil-speaking Indians in a way that makes little sense when we speak of Australians, Americans, or Germans.

It is these linguistic and cultural characteristics that, when formalized, can become the basis for national-type identities. I am using the term *national* in the sociological sense that was advanced in chapter 1, where reference was made to communities with historical features, shared cultural values, and aspirations to a common destiny. The term does not by itself entail sovereign statehood.

Yet there is potential ambiguity surrounding the status of national communities within federations. Under certain circumstances, they may well dream of independence; they may remember (or imagine) some long-forgotten past when they were not associated with their present co-citizens; they may feel that coercion, rather than free will, has led to their current status; or they may think that for economic, political, or cultural reasons they would be better off on their own than bound up with the larger political unit.

At a minimum, therefore, multinational federations must make particular efforts to ensure that the interests of the federation and of its different national components are in harmony. One way is by ensuring a fair degree of autonomy to each of the constituent units, especially in linguistic and cultural matters, but perhaps in social and economic ones, as well. This approach seems to be the one Switzerland has adopted, with additional provisions whereby citizens are guaranteed, through referenda and initiatives, the final say on all important matters.

Yet Switzerland was not always a model of civic harmony and light, as the Sonderbund war fought between Catholic cantons and the rest of the country in the middle of the 19th century would suggest. Switzerland's geopolitical position at the centre of Europe adjacent to Germany and France, its mountainous terrain, its traditional neutrality may, nonetheless, have helped reinforce internal cohesion. Neither the French nor German nor Italian cantons would have necessarily fared better independently. But neither would Switzerland have survived had one of the major communities, for example, the German, simply lorded it over the others.

Another way of keeping multinational federations together is through brute force reinforced by the appeal of ideology. The Soviet Union stands as the striking example of this in our century. Marxist-Leninism, Soviet-style, was prepared to acknowledge the principle of nationality, to constitute the postrevolutionary state on a federal basis, to even endorse the right to secession for its constituent republics in such texts as the 1936 constitution. On the other hand, it did no better than the tsars when it came to allowing these republics real autonomy. Communist ideology and the Communist Party of the Soviet Union, in particular, left little place for initiatives from the republics. Nationalist tendencies were systematically suppressed, by armed force as in the Ukraine or the Caucasus in the early years of the regime, by purges, or by population displacement and transfers. The Russian element, by dint of numbers, economic and political strength, and linguistic and cultural prestige, overrode all others.

Under the surface, in songs and samizdat, alternative visions of national community persisted. And to a certain degree, the official nationality policy of the regime did give legitimacy to at least language and certain forms of culture in the different republics and autonomous regions. But the long-term goal, articulated most clearly during the Brezhnev period, was the fusion of the different nationalities into a single Soviet amalgam. Overall, there was little that was genuinely federal about the operation of the Soviet Union when compared to other federal states.

Of course, everything changed during the period of glasnost and perestroika and far more quickly than even Soviet reformers might have expected. For once the iron hand of the party had been lifted, the centre rapidly lost its grip in the republics; national sentiment, long suppressed, came to the surface. While the goal that Mikhail Gorbachev set himself in 1990–91 seemed like a perfectly commendable one — a looser confederal arrangement among the republics with, however, a common structure for foreign affairs, defence, and international trade — it came after 70-odd years of extreme centralization. There was little trust in the other republics for the Russian big brother, with the Baltic States and the Ukraine leading the way toward independence. The Commonwealth of Independent States, set up in December 1991 to link 11 of the former republics, had no effective clout.

Other multinational federations fall somewhere between the Swiss and Soviet extremes. Yugoslavia, for example, was established as a union of Slovenes, Croats, and Serbs in the aftermath of World War I. It was not a forced union, although the Serb element dominated until World War II. The Nazi occupation saw atrocities committed on all sides, but with the Croats more guilty on this score than the Serbs. In Tito's Yugoslavia, the League of Communists played much the same role as the Communist Party of the Soviet Union in keeping the country together. Yet the republics were granted significantly greater autonomy than in the Soviet Union, in economic no less than in cultural matters. The death of Tito and the subsequent collapse of communism in Eastern Europe produced a rapid meltdown of the Yugoslav state. The tragedy of Yugoslavia, however, lay not only in a legacy of hatred dating back to World War II and before, but in the noncorrespondence of political boundaries and ethnic populations, especially in the cases of Croatia, Bosnia-Herzegovina, and Serbia itself.

With the power both of communism and the central government removed, the stage was set for a bitter settling of accounts. Slovenia's independence was one thing, Croatia's another. It took a year of conflict to bring about the de facto severance of Serb-inhabited or occupied territory from the rest of Croatia. In the case of Bosnia-Herzegovina, the politics of ethnicity was even more tangled, with no one group constituting a clear majority within the republic. Brutal civil war with support from both Serbia and Croatia for their respective ethnic communities ensued, leading to near-total partition of Bosnia and mass expulsion of Muslims from Serb- and Croat-controlled territories. Repeated protestations from the European Community and the United Nations fell on deaf ears. Within Serbia the region of Kosovo with its 90 percent Albanian majority is kept on the tightest of leashes. Its revolt would touch off a larger conflagration throughout the Balkans.

It is easy to play prophet after the event. But one cannot help asking oneself whether the people of Yugoslavia — millions of displaced people and hundreds of thousands of dead and wounded later — would not be better off today had the forces of meltdown stopped short of complete independence after 1989. The principle of nationality for the different republics could have been recognized within a looser Yugoslav confederation in which each of the republics would have secured maximum autonomy; minority rights could have been negotiated and secured; and ethnic minorities would not have been forced to adopt the citizenship of the separate republics.

The mere fact that such a solution did not prove attractive to Slovenia or Croatia underlines how tainted the federal nature of Yugoslavia had become in the eyes of certain of its nationalities. Having enjoyed, from their point of view, insufficient autonomy over the previous decades, dreaming perhaps of sovereign flags, armies, and economic relations with the West, their populations were less prepared to envisage even a loose framework with the other republics. The historical forces at work in the Balkans, moreover, made the kind of give-and-take necessary for a federation along Swiss lines much less attainable.

A federal system for Czechs and Slovaks had been established in January 1969 in the aftermath of the Warsaw Pact suppression of the Prague Spring, which was a black period in the country's history and an ominous moment for such initiatives. For the very Communist power that was repressing liberalization and reform was, for cynical reasons of its own, prepared to grant Soviet-style recognition to the existence of the two major national groupings.

The roots of Slovak nationalism, of course, predate the Communist period. There was an element of tension between Slovaks and Czechs during the first republic of 1918–39, but as with Yugoslavia, World War II brought home major cleavages, with the Slovaks (or their elites) by and large collaborating with the Nazis, and the Czechs more directly paying the price of Munich. Some of these differences would never be put to rest despite 40 years of Communist rule.

The aftermath of the Velvet Revolution of November 1989 saw the renaming of the state as the Federal Republic of Czechs and Slovaks. Although the Slovaks had secured a functioning parliament and government of their own, they pressed for even greater autonomy. There was also a significant difference between the two republics regarding the pace of market reform. Parliamentary elections in June 1992 brought things to a head, with a strongly nationalist government elected in Slovakia and a free market-oriented Czech government in Prague. The latter showed little inclination to work out some looser federal or confederal arrangement with the Slovaks, preferring a complete rupture. The decision to separate was taken by the governing parties of the two republics without submitting it to the population for approval by referendum. Decades of shared repression did not leave behind sufficient goodwill to make a voluntary type of federation function.

Where then do other multinational federations such as India, Belgium, or Canada fit into this analysis? My temptation is to put them somewhat closer to the Swiss than to the Soviet pole, but with a question mark as to how well or poorly they will hang together into the future.

In the case of India, partition occurred in 1947 with the carving of a separate Pakistan out of the largely Muslim regions of the northeast and northwest. The existence of religious cleavages, along with other divisions such as caste, has served in a way to make the linguistic and cultural divisions across state lines less acute. (In similar fashion, it has been argued that the Catholic–Protestant division in Switzerland, by not simply mirroring the German–French one, serves as a unifying factor.)

Yet India has known secessionist movements over the years. There was one in what is now Tamil Nadu in the south in the late 1950s and 1960s when a political party, the DMK, aiming at independence, came to the fore. It was eventually able to achieve some of its objectives as a state government, but it also had to deal with the heavy hand of New Delhi where presidential rule and the possibility of military intervention were concerned.

A more severe threat to Indian unity arose in the Punjab in the 1970s. A conjunction of language and religion, economic and political grievances vis-à-vis the centre and the neighbouring state of Himachal Pradesh, and radicalization of the Sikh-based Akali Dal Party, brought matters to a boil. Armed intervention by the central government at the Golden Temple at Amritsar did not end the unrest; the then prime minister of India, Indira Gandhi, paid for the suppression of Sikh nationalism with her life. There have also been tribal insurgencies in states like Assam, and there is persistent sentiment among the majority Muslim population of Kashmir for unification with Pakistan. So India potentially sits atop a volcano where nationality issues are concerned.

Unlike the Soviet Union, however, there have been provisions for a fair degree of state autonomy in matters like culture, education, land distribution, or social programs, and a drawing (or redrawing) of state lines to better correspond to linguistic and ethnic groupings. The result has been a greater possibility of containing national sentiment of a sociological sort within the framework of the Indian union. And there are the further factors of common struggle — across linguistic and cultural lines — for independence from Britain, as well as rivalry with Pakistan since independence, to help keep most centrifugal forces at bay. Any attempt, however, to override linguistic and cultural differences, say, through imposition of Hindi from the centre, or to impose greater centralization of power in New Delhi, could spark explosions.

For a long time, Belgium was a unitary state, created out of the largely Catholic part of the Low Countries in 1830 to serve as a political buffer with the support of the great powers. Throughout the 19th century, its dominant political and economic establishment was French-speaking, with Flanders something of a backwater. Linguistically French speakers tended to look down on Flemish as a second-rate language.

The 20th century was to bring profound change, with a decline in the coal-mining Walloon regions and the emergence of a more entrepreneurial class in Flanders. Belgium, too, was to experience Nazi occupation, with the Flemish, by and large, more inclined to tolerate the Germans than the Walloons. There had been a fascist movement, the Rexists, of some size in Flanders in the 1930s, and the Belgian monarch, Leopold III, unlike his Dutch counterpart, remained at home throughout the war. A plebiscite on his future in 1950 split the country, with the Flemish voting for his retention and the Walloons for his removal. Only Leopold's abdication the following year in favour of his son Baudouin saved the country from a more serious political crisis.

Over the post-World War II period, the two linguistic communities have grown increasingly farther apart. There have been major conflicts over the linguistic status of Brussels and its suburbs, over the exact location of the language boundary down the middle of the country, and over the future of an institution like the University of Louvain, resulting in its splintering into two. The Flemish, the larger of the two communities and the more prosperous today, have taken revenge on the Walloons for their earlier domination, and the Walloons have become more alienated from central institutions in which the Flemish have a permanent majority.

Linguistic nationalism has served to undercut a common Belgian identity. Belgium, as a result, has experimented with federal institutions, devolving ever-greater power to the two linguistic regions; it remains to be seen exactly what functions other than foreign affairs or defence will remain in the hands of the Belgian state by the year 2000. Even as the European Community, headquartered in Brussels, supposedly brings Europeans closer together, Belgium may opt for a more decentralizing route than Switzerland. The only other alternative seems to be complete breakup.

Returning to Canada and our own dilemmas as a multinational federation, I would argue that English Canadians tend to interpret Canadian history along consensual and democratic lines. They see Confederation as the result of free choice among the British North American colonies, and view Quebec as having had ample opportunity to develop freely ever since. But in Quebec the picture can be seen quite differently. There is an act of coercion that marks the joining of Quebec to Canada, namely, the British conquest of New France. There was the suppression of the rebellion of 1837–38. There was something less than free and frank popular approval of Confederation in 1867 — it was never submitted to the population as such. There was permanent minority status for Quebec at the federal level — as was brought home clearly enough with the introduction of conscription during two world wars. Such views colour the history texts in Quebec and the self-perceptions of Quebec nationalists.

The theme of an earlier French-Canadian nationalism, *la surviv-ance* or survival, lives on in a fashion in contemporary Quebec nationalism. And with it — who can deny it? — comes a certain desire to settle old scores. The passion surrounding the official status of French in Quebec — Bills 22, 101, and 178, for example — reminds one of the Belgian situation. Only vigorous legislative intervention by the government of Quebec, so the nationalist argument goes, can ensure a dominant role for French in the one and only French-language jurisdiction in North America. Symbolically, at the same time, such laws help to undo the painful legacy of anglophone domination over the Quebec economy, over the public spaces of a city like Montreal, over the very French-Canadian psyche.

The community of destiny to which Quebec nationalists appeal is the community of Quebec. Where once religion played a determining role in cementing French-Canadian identity, today it is far more clearly language. Where once the demand was for strict observance of the division of powers outlined in sections 91 and 92 of the British North America Act, now the call is for significantly greater jurisdictional powers for Quebec.

It does not follow from this that a majority of Québécois feel no Canadian affinity whatsoever, or that the history of Quebec within Canada has simply been one of crude oppression. If this were the case, there would have been overwhelming support for Quebec sovereignty in the referendum of 1980, much as there was for Ukrainian or Lithuanian or Slovenian independence in referenda held in those republics a decade later. There would have been a 75 to 80 percent No vote in the October 1992 referendum, or a corresponding share of the vote in favour of the Bloc Québécois in October 1993.

Ambiguity is the hallmark of minority national sentiment within multinational federations. There is the desire for recognition as a distinctive linguistic and cultural community within any such state, and for a large measure of autonomy to give that distinctiveness expression. But there may well be historical, geopolitical, economic, and other reasons to continue to live within a common state structure. It would be strange indeed if a century and more of cohabitation had not sparked some common sentiments among the different linguistic groups that make up a federation such as Canada, above and beyond their separate national identities.

We in Canada do not have the experience of coercive centralization of the Tsarist or Soviet regimes, nor do we have the blood hatreds that seem to characterize the Serb–Croat, Armenian–Azeri, Georgian–Abkhaz relationships. Furthermore, we are prepared to respect cultural differences within some ongoing federal or possibly confederal framework in which democratic principles are the norm. As such, there is greater hope for our multinational federation than there was for those that have recently succumbed.

But nothing is certain. Canadians have not only the question of Quebec to address. We also need to take aboriginal people into account. And we need to start addressing a question that has lurked beneath the surface until now but whose resolution lies at the very heart of our current predicament, namely, the national status of the majority English-speaking group.

What is English Canada? Are its inhabitants prepared to see themselves as constituting a cultural community/nationality in the way that members of minority nationalities see themselves? Do they have a rigid or an open attitude toward the type of political institutions required to make a multinational federation work?

The principal lesson to be drawn from the recent meltdown of other multinational federations is crystal clear. One can attempt to repress national sentiments with the near certainty that these will blow up at such point as the powers of coercion weaken or disappear. Or one can attempt to allay national differences by so structuring such federations as to allow maximum autonomy and self-expression to each of the national components. In post-Meech, post-Charlottetown Canada, English Canadians can contribute to the process of political renewal by boldly confronting what we have for so long sought to elude, namely, the nature and raison d'être of our own national community.

3

English Canada as Sociological Nation

THE VERY TERM *English Canada* seems to strike a false note. Does the word *English* refer to ethnic origin or to country of origin? If so, less than 40 percent of the population of Canada as a whole and less than 50 percent of the population of Canada outside Quebec would qualify. The term would exclude ten million or more Canadians of non-British background (quite aside from the slur to those of Scottish, Welsh, or Irish background) and threaten to establish a hierarchy of first-class versus second-class citizens. No wonder many, whether first-generation or tenth-generation Canadians, might find the term objectionable.

If by English Canada one really means English-speaking Canada, the term is somewhat more acceptable. The vast majority of the population of Canada outside Quebec, regardless of ethnic origin, does use English as its primary means of communication. It is the language of education, commerce, politics, sports, and everyday life for all but first-generation immigrants and minority language enclaves. Yet even *English-speaking* begs the question of official language minorities — namely, the half-million to a million Franco-Canadians outside Quebec, many of whom retain some attachment to French, and the half-million to three-quarter-million Anglo-Quebeckers, for whom English is the first language. Are English Canada and English-speaking Canada one and the same thing?

There is a third sense in which we could use the term. We would be referring neither to ethnic origin nor to language *in abstracto*, but to culture and territory. The culture in question would be the *largely* English-language culture of Canada to which those of diverse ethnic origins have contributed; and the territory in question would be the very extensive terrain, essentially outside Quebec and populated by nonaboriginals, that has English speakers as its dominant grouping.

Used in this sense, English Canada would logically have French Canada as its counterpart. This latter term, however, has usually referred not only to Quebec (minus its anglophone minority), but to the French-speaking areas of New Brunswick, Ontario, et cetera, as well. It emanates from the post-Confederation period and highlights an underlying duality between English and French long held to exist across the country.

But sociological, much like political terms, are not innocent. The term *French Canada* has ceased to be a term of self-identification where a majority of francophone Quebeckers are concerned; it has been replaced by the more potent and territorially specific term *Québécois*. This term, when used in nationalist discourse, encompasses Anglo-Quebeckers, allophones, and Quebec aboriginals, but excludes the francophone population of the rest of Canada.

As *French Canada* has tended to fall by the wayside, why would *English Canada* become a term of self-identification elsewhere? Does it not threaten to throw Quebec anglophones, most of whom oppose Quebec nationalism, to the sovereigntist wolves? Does it not make light of the multicultural contribution to 20th-century Canada, thereby buying into a concept of duality that is dead and gone? Does it not raise difficult problems where minority language rights for francophones may be concerned? And does it not open up a political Pandora's box when the question of who speaks for *English Canada* is posed? No wonder few have been prepared to embark into such a minefield.

Do we really have a choice? Not only does a majority of Québécois francophones (and by no means all sovereigntists) define Quebec as a nation, but we are witnessing similar assertions on the part of aboriginal peoples. We can reject these assertions, stonewall, or attempt, à la Charlottetown, to paper over some of the hard institutional consequences that would accompany any such recognition. If what I have previously been arguing about multinational federations, however, is correct, we have everything to gain from embracing, rather than spurning, the term *English Canada.*

To begin with, it is not a purely artificial construct. At a common-sense, everyday level, Canadians, from the time of Confederation onward, have distinguished between English and French Canadians. Language has been a primary criterion; religion, for a long time, another; political identification or nonidentification with the British empire yet a third. It made sense to explain the tension surrounding the hanging of Louis Riel as one between French Canada and English. The same would be true regarding minority language rights in Manitoba and Ontario, Canadian involvement in the Boer War, the financing of dreadnoughts for the British navy, and military partici-pation in both world wars. Seldom, in fact, did Canada seem closer to breakup than over the question of conscription in the two wars.

But what was this *English Canada* that seemed at loggerheads with *French Canada?* Certainly it was not a formal political entity with a governmental structure of its own, nor was it a political party, although the Conservatives, in their more Tory, pro-British incarna-tion, often came closer to embodying it than the Liberals. And nor was it even the provinces with anglophone majorities — as crucial as Ontario was, in particular, in helping to formulate the leading version of English-Canadian opinion.

English Canada was a set of communities with certain common affinities, stemming partly from origin, primarily in the British Isles, partly from a shared political structure — the Dominion of Canada. There were close similarities with the founding colonists of the United States, not surprising given the importance of Loyalist migra-tion in the aftermath of the American Revolution. The British strain was more salient, however, reinforced by continuing migration from the British Isles throughout the 19th century and into the 20th.

This British element was particularly influential in marking the underlying ethos of Canadian society. At the religious level, this meant a mixture of High Church and Low Church traditions, for example, Anglican with Presbyterian and Methodist, and something of that sense of divine favour accorded a people both devout and enterprising. Religious toleration had its place, but a certain suspi-cion toward Catholics and others was prevalent for a long time. At the political level, it meant an emphasis on the values of stability, moderation, and timely reform, in different degrees, and an acceptance of the British constitution — king/queen-in-Parliament and the common law — lock, stock, and barrel. The founding doctrine of 1867 can be traced back directly to it. At a more mythic level, British influence made itself felt in identification with the British empire, with Anglo-Saxon cultural superiority — Rudyard Kipling and all that — and with the economic ascendancy of British capitalism.

That Canada was a new society in North America did, however, serve to modify the picture. Canada's was a hard frontier; the tyranny of both climate and distance would thrust a significant role on the state in nation-building. The population-to-land ratio was low, compounded by out-migration from Canada to the United States. The gates to non-British immigration would need to be opened, however reluctantly, if the West especially were to be settled. Furthermore, the presence of a dynamic and expansive republic to the south and of an unassimilated French-speaking population within would make it more difficult for a purely Anglo- or British-Canadian vision of society to win out.

Overall, English Canada, particularly in the 20th century, would become a more diffuse and pluralistic type of society than the one of which Loyalists or the Orange Lodges had dreamed. The decline in Britain's world role had something to do with it; the United States had a democratizing influence on Canadian political culture; new sources of immigration from continental Europe to the Far East would play an important part. These and other transformations have made the search for an English-Canadian identity an elusive one.

There are derivative characteristics, as in British influence on political structures and economic development during the first 50 to 75 years of Canada's existence as a country; or in American influence on the economy, foreign and defence policies, mass media, and popular culture for much of the 20th century; or in the different cultural traditions that scores of ethnic communities have brought with them from elsewhere. What, one might ask, is specifically *Canadian* about English Canada?

Then there is the problem of disentangling the *English-Canadian* from the pan-Canadian dimension when we speak about broad features of Canadian development, or in being able to generalize meaningfully about what may often appear as regionally specific patterns. What is English Canada above and beyond the Atlantic provinces, English Quebec (or is it even included?), Ontario, the Prairies, British Columbia, and the territories?

The task before us appears formidable, all the more if we are expected to chronicle every nook and cranny of the English-Canadian psyche. Perhaps, then, we can permit ourselves a shortcut, recognizing along with contemporary students of nationalism like Benedict Anderson that there is an element of imagined community at work in defining nationalities. What elements might we want to emphasize in imagining English Canada?

1) Language and culture are defining characteristics of any national grouping. The language of English Canada — recent immigrants and minorities like Acadians or Franco-Ontarians aside — is English. This, at least, is one unifying element, accent and dialect notwithstanding, from Bonavista to Vancouver Island; it differentiates English Canada from francophone Quebec. That English Canadians share this same language with the United States, Great Britain, Australia, New Zealand, et cetera, is another matter to which we shall subsequently want to return. For the moment, it is the clearest defining characteristic of English Canada to which we can point.

By comparison, culture is a more amorphous construct. What place, for example, does religion have in the framing of English-Canadian culture? A good deal, if we are looking at the Canada of a century or more ago when religious values marked education and civic culture at all levels. Even 50 years ago, religious influence was more than passing on our political system — witness parties like the Cooperative Commonwealth Federation (CCF) and Social Credit — and in terms of sexual mores, family practice, censorship, and the like. Today, as well, there are significant numbers of English Canadians — not all fundamentalists, by any means — who find in religion the values that bind.

In all sorts of ways, however, English Canada, like other Western societies, has become much more secular. Industrialization and urbanization have worked their effects. So, too, have ever higher levels of education, not to mention technological innovations like the pill. Religion, of course, has not entirely vanished from people's lives: at ritualistic moments like birth, marriage, death, or holidays, it may return with a vengeance. But it is at best one value among many rather than a primordial one. Moreover, the range of acceptable religious practices is much larger today — from mainstream Christian denominations or fundamentalist ones to non-Christian religions, New Age, and no religion at all — than would have been true in 19th-century English Canada.

How much weight ought we, then, to put on other cultural factors? High-brow culture like theatre, film, art, novels, poetry? Media like the CBC? Newspapers and magazines? Sports? Community-based institutions from libraries to a myriad of voluntary associations?

Clearly these factors do matter. Some may indeed cater to minority tastes, while helping to shape a specifically English-Canadian sensibility. Others, like public education (which many may not even think of as cultural), have served to socialize a large majority of English Canadians through the generations to a national consciousness. Still others such as hockey have come to incarnate a national myth, transcending the linguistic boundary.

That there has been a great deal of direct American influence on most aspects of English-Canadian culture, especially popular culture, is undeniable. That there has been anguished concern about this in various quarters over the decades, namely, the League for Canadian Broadcasting, the Massey Commission, the Committee for an Independent Canada, is equally undeniable. The upshot has been the typically (English) Canadian solution of state support for key cultural and scientific activities — broadcasting, the performing arts, literature, research in the natural and social sciences. English-Canadian culture, as a result, has enjoyed fairly dramatic development over the past 50 or 60 years. And at some levels we have met one of the great challenges of modernity — how to live successfully cheek by jowl with the United States and survive. Whether this specifically Canadian cultural activity provides sufficient counterweight to American influence in helping to shape the English-Canadian psyche is, of course, open to debate. Whether the lessons we have learned from past experience will carry over into the next century also remains to be seen.

2) A second characteristic of the English-Canadian *imaginaire* is territory or space. What sets Canada apart from others on the globe is the particular territory it occupies in the northern part of North America, the three oceans — Atlantic, Pacific, and Arctic — that it touches, the mythos of harsh climate, endless winter, tundra, and shield with which Canadians like to regale themselves.

For a long time, geography served as a substitute for history. Not only was history on the English-Canadian side (outside the Maritimes) relatively new, dating from after 1759, but it seemed rather undramatic when compared to the national histories of the United States, France, or Great Britain. True, there was the War of 1812; an ill-fated attempt at popular rebellion in 1837 that came to naught; and (English) Canadian participation, with no small sacrifice of lives, in two world wars. But the events of mainstream Canadian history, Confederation included, were relatively tame affairs. Nor would 20th-century Canadians, particularly those of non-British origin, find much in this earlier history to excite them. Canadian geography, by comparison, was unique and challenging.

Yet geography itself has become a potentially contested domain. Is the geography of English Canada the same thing as the physical geography of Canada as a whole? Or do the claims of both Québécois and aboriginal peoples to nationhood force us to rethink matters?

English Canada certainly includes the Atlantic provinces, but does the Acadian portion of New Brunswick fit in quite the same way as the rest? It might well include, at the cultural level at least, the anglophone portions of Quebec, confined though these are to bits of the Eastern Townships, the West Island of Montreal, and the Outaouais. But could it include these *politically* when Quebec as a whole might in important ways come to define itself differently from the rest of Canada? This is highly unlikely. How solid, for that matter, would the map from the Ottawa River west and north to the Arctic Circle appear? Here and there would be minority francophone communities; more conspicuously still, an archipelago of aboriginal communities would crisscross the length and breadth of Canada's territory. Potentially much of northern Canada would be aboriginal land. Suddenly we would find ourselves face-to-face with unexpected landscapes, like travellers to Italo Calvino's imaginary cities. Is the English-Canadian psyche ready for the shock?

3) Perhaps it is. A striking feature of English-Canadian society is its spirit of live and let live. English Canadians are not a passionately political people, driven by the demons and furies of many Old World and Third World societies. Nationalism under most circumstances, world wars aside, is of a circumspect variety, bespeaking a somewhat diffident attitude toward the larger powers with whom we have been engaged. There is a good deal less of the ethnic hatred that we see elsewhere; as between English and French, for example, the spirit of the Royal Commission on Bilingualism and Biculturalism and of the Official Languages Act comes closer to capturing the contemporary English-Canadian attitude than the assimilationist views of the Durham Report of old. Aboriginals have acquired a new, more favourable status in English-Canadian public opinion as a people to whom injustice has been committed in the past; as for immigrants, the prevailing mode of mosaic, rather than melting pot, is at least testament to openness.

The above lines are not meant to sanction sins of omission and commission in our past. Aboriginal peoples have a documented history of repression and cultural brainwashing at the hands of whites; French-language minorities were in a weak and vulnerable position in English Canada when compared to that of Quebec's anglophone minority; derogatory attitudes toward bohunks and "inferior races," along with barriers to nonwhite immigration, reflected an uglier side of English-Canadian attitudes over time; the forced relocation of Japanese Canadians during World War II or closed-door policy toward Jews fleeing Nazi Europe in the 1930s further blots the record.

Nonetheless, English Canada today is, broadly speaking, a pluralistic and polyethnic society that does not subscribe to a single founding myth. Nor is there a single charter group, for instance, those of British stock, lording it in a way that still seemed true when John Porter was writing his classic *The Vertical Mosaic* in the early 1960s. The accession of first- and third- and fifth-generation Canadians of non-British origin to key positions in the political, economic, professional, and cultural hierarchies of English-Canadian society is one of the great transformations of our time. The position of women, while well short of complete equality with men where political representation, earning power, or representation in the social order are concerned, is significantly better than in the recent past; for this development, feminism can take some deserved credit. English-Canadian society is also more open to demands for equality of treatment by previously silent groups, such as visible minorities, people with disabilities, gays and lesbians, than before. And there is, as already suggested, a fairly positive attitude toward aboriginal people unlike anything in our past.

I am not here making unnecessary claims to virtue or benefi-cence — English Canadians, had they found themselves caught up in bitter territorial rivalries like other peoples, might well have acted in the same way. We have thus far been spared the test by both geography and history. So that to emphasize tolerance as a cardinal principle of English Canada is a simple observation of fact, not a testament to moral superiority or hard prediction about the future.

4) Canada, in contrast to the United States, is not founded on the notion of "life, liberty, and the pursuit of happiness"; nor, in contrast to France, on that of "liberty, equality, fraternity." To the degree that an analogous formula is said to exist for this country, it is usually "peace, order, and good government" of section 91 of the British North America Act.

In probing the basis of English Canada, we need to go beyond such ritualistic formulae. There has been a broadening and deepening of the English-Canadian political tradition since 1867; at the same time, there has been a universalization of the basic values of liberal democ-racy, in the post-1945 period especially, to a point where specific national derivations matter less than real-life practices.

English Canada is the heir, in varying degrees, to three major political currents of our century: the conservative, the liberal, and the social democratic. Each has contributed something unique to the *Weltgeist* or spirit of English-Canadian society.

For a long time, the conservative element was, indeed, associated with authority. It was at the heart of an earlier counterrevolutionary ethos — quite consciously opposed to the Americans with their republicanism and armed break from Britain, given instead to veneration of monarchy, aristocracy, and acquired wealth. The road to an English-Canadian identity lay in and through the British empire, and in values associated with governance in the British mould. Representative institutions capped by dignified symbols — governor general/lieutenant governor — were the constitutional summum bonum of such thinking; protectionism with a touch of state enterprise, the embodiment of economic thinking; participation at the side of Britain in world wars, the fulfillment of kinship obligations. Inevitably the content of conservatism has changed through the post-World War II period, our American half century, to something more closely aligned with free market economics and North American values. Elements of an earlier conservative ethos as regards symbols of authority like courts or the Royal Canadian Mounted Police have, however, persisted.

The liberal element has been more inclined to celebrate liberty than order and to push the case for reforms. In some ways, it was more firmly North American-rooted than conservatism, less given to the cult of things British. Strongly supportive of business capitalism, it, nonetheless, accepted the need for accommodation of labour. It also came, by mid-20th century, to be associated with both Keynesianism and elements of the welfare state. Sensitivity toward Quebec and toward multiculturalism are also strands, as is, in the most recent period, an emphasis on individual rights as exemplified in the Charter of Rights and Freedoms. To the degree, in fact, that there is a liberal vision of English Canada today, it would be a rights-based one.

The social democratic element, historically, has been more minoritarian than the other two. It came later than conservatism and liberalism and, with social democracy largely absent in the United States, has had a harder time of it in Canada. Yet key elements of English-Canadian identity, from cultural institutions like the CBC to social programs like medicare have their roots in the endeavours of social democratically-minded individuals and governments. In a larger sense, social democracy speaks to a more community-minded, collectivist pole in the English-Canadian psyche, one which serves to balance off purely individualistic elements.

A thesis to which I will return in chapter 4 is that we must not see each of these in total isolation; rather, there has been significant cross-fertilization of ideas and values in English-Canadian society to a point where the latter embodies an interesting blend of conservativism, liberalism, and social democracy. This may well be one of English Canada's more original features.

5) A major problem in grappling with English Canada is its regional diversity. We do not begin with an abstract entity called English Canada; once we go below the level of Canada as we know it today, the not unnatural tendency is to think in terms of region. Our very geographical heterogeneity might make some despair of piecing together a coherent nationality out of the fragments.

There are two ways to deal with this problem. One is to deny it by emphasizing instead the commonalities that English-speaking Canadians share after more than 125 years of living within a single-state structure. The other is to recognize that regional perspectives have coloured visions of nation and country in the past; it should therefore come as no surprise that the same would be true for any English-Canadian nationality we try to imagine.

Canada, if we think things through, would have been a federal state even if Quebec had never existed. It is not the French–English division alone that led to the federal arrangements of 1867. The Maritime colonies were reluctant participants in a venture where central Canada threatened to overwhelm them, and provincial autonomy was the sine qua non for their adherence to Confederation, with Prince Edward Island holding out until 1873 and Newfoundland until 1949! The West, as it came to be settled, was even more resentful of economic and political control from the East. No centralized structure along European lines would have been able to keep a continent-wide state of Canada's size and far-flung population together for long.

Regionalism, then, is a constituent feature of English Canada. Geographical markers — oceans, rivers, lakes, prairies, mountains, tundra — serve to delineate boundaries; primary resources and economic activities set provinces and regions apart; political culture — old parties versus new, populist versus nonpopulist, right, centre, or left — further varies with provincial lines.

Granting all these factors, we might then ask: Is there sufficient sense of common values, shared history and, most of all, the desire to function as a nation in the hearts of English Canadians to surmount regional differences? Would such common sentiments survive the shock of a renegotiated relationship with Quebec, for example, asymmetrical federalism, confederal arrangements, or sovereignty with or without association?

The likely answer to both of these is "Yes, but." Just as regions and provinces provide a significant part of English Canadians' sense of identity, so, in a crucial way, does our shared experience as a federal state. Much in English Canada's political reflexes, economic infrastructure, and cultural attitudes is associated with the role and activities of the federal government. The National Policy and railway construction, the Wheat Board and the CBC, participation in world wars or in U.N. peacekeeping operations, social security programs or the flag, have been defining characteristics of our identity. The federal government has not been an alien government for a majority of English Canadians in a way that Quebec nationalists purport to see it. On the contrary, it is absolutely central to any ongoing English-Canadian nationality.

This attitude, incidentally, explains some of the opposition in English Canada to both the Meech and Charlottetown accords and the resonance that Pierre Trudeau's views in particular have had. There is a significant body of English-Canadian opinion that would oppose any gutting of the federal government. That same body of opinion would fight hard to maintain a common national structure against forces of wholesale devolution *within* English Canada.

There is, therefore, potential conflict between more provincially oriented and more federally oriented visions of nationality within English Canada. Such a tug of war need not prove fatal. Advocates of strong federal powers can no more deny the legitimacy of region and province than could the Fathers of Confederation; the provincially minded, if they do not want a hollow shell for a country, will similarly have to accept that a nation is more than the sum of its parts. The court of judgement as to where the balance ought to lie will be English-Canadian public opinion.

Any change in Quebec's status would bring home with some urgency the existential question facing English Canadians — "To be or not to be." One possible reaction would indeed be to go for a looser association of provinces or regions within English Canada. But the counterargument, potentially quite potent in a period of crisis, would be the need to reinforce bonds within English Canada in order to survive. Not only would there be the question of redefining relations with Quebec, but the old fears that stoked an earlier Canadian nationalism, namely absorption into the United States, would be reawakened.

The question of region, nonetheless, underlines the need for great creativity in conceptualizing English Canada. Besides questions of balance among and between the different regions and provinces, there would have to be a place for the diversity of perspectives and lived histories that make up the different regions of the country. Otherwise there will be no English Canada.

6) Finally brief reference must be made to one other element in the English-Canadian *imaginaire* — our view of our place in the world. In some ways, when we focus on our internal debates, Canadians can appear quite parochial; yet at other points, as in our participation in international organizations such as the United Nations, the Commonwealth, and NATO, there is a strongly internationalist current at work.

This internationalism is by no means limited to governmental actors. One thinks of Canadian churches and their role in spearheading opposition to apartheid; of environmental organizations like Greenpeace, which had their origins in Canada and have gone on to play an important international role; of the Canadian involvement in Oxfam, Amnesty International, CUSO, and a host of other similar agencies.

English Canadians have few illusions about living on an island unto themselves. This goes far beyond the questions of trade and investment that the business community and its friends in government are always highlighting; it extends to the shape of the larger international system, to questions of north-south relations, human rights, democracy, social justice, and much else.

There is, in the English-Canadian temperament, as earlier suggested, a reticence to embrace nationalism in its more fulsome, extroverted forms. This characteristic explains some of the difficulty in comparing English Canada with Quebec or the United States. However, this reticence may be something of an advantage when it comes to defining our place in the larger international system. It helps give English Canadians a sense of identity as a nation with a commitment to making international organizations work. Perhaps this is a healthier basis for defining nationality on the eve of the 21st century than by casting about for Jungian archetypes in the collective unconscious. Increasingly, being good international citizens may be part of what being good citizens of any particular country is about. In this respect, English Canadians are off to a good start.

4

English-Canadian Political Culture

L ET US NOW LOOK IN SEQUENCE at the three currents in English-Canadian political culture referred to in the previous chapter, namely conservatism, liberalism, and social democracy.

The Conservative Strain

At one level, the conservative strain is the most familiar current, yet it is also the most distant. Many Canadians would buy into George Grant/Louis Hartz/Gad Horowitz arguments about a Tory touch to English-Canadian society. It is our lack of a founding liberal ideology resplendent with the terminology of the Declaration of Independence or the American Constitution that sets us off from our neighbour to the south. Ours was a more ordered and more peaceful society; our emancipation from Great Britain a matter of slow, incremental change rather than revolutionary upsurge.

If one wants a name to associate with this form of conservatism, one is tempted to invoke that of Edmund Burke. Although he wrote in Great Britain in the latter part of the 18th century, something of his spirit was alive in Canadian Toryism. His was a strong defence of English liberties as opposed to the abstract rights invoked by the revolutionaries in France; a defence of the independence of MPs from undue control by their electors; a defence of privilege and property within a context of ordered change; a veneration of tradition in a world of shifting sands; a prudentially positive attitude toward the state; an openness to commerce and industry with a hint of paternalism toward the lower orders.

In what sense can we speak of similar strains in English Canada down to World War II? One aspect of English-Canadian conservatism, it has sometimes been argued, lay in a willingness to use the state, both as an instrument of protectionism and as public entrepreneur of the last resort. The Conservatives were more attached to high tariffs and imperial preference than their Liberal counterparts. At the same time, ventures like Ontario Hydro established in 1908 by a provincial Conservative government or the CNR by Robert Borden's federal government in 1918 and, in a related vein, R. B. Bennett's radio addresses of January 1935 bespoke an openness to state enterprise and intervention.

Another aspect lay in a proneness to repression faced with any challenge to authority. This tendency was most evident in the deployment of the militia in Winnipeg in 1919 at the time of the General Strike, or again of the army in Regina in 1935 to head off the Trek on Ottawa. It further surfaced in the use of the Criminal Code to suppress Communist activity in the early 1930s. The Russian Revolution was for Canadian Conservatives what the French Revolution had been to Burke.

Yet a third aspect lay in the wholesale rejection of any forms of direct democracy, be it the initiative, recall, or referendum. The Conservative opposition in Manitoba was successful in getting a provincial bill providing for initiatives ruled ultra vires by the Judicial Committee of the Privy Council in 1919. In Ottawa, the Borden government withstood repeated calls from the Liberal opposition for a referendum on conscription in 1917, arguing that this would be foreign to British parliamentary practice. Legitimacy lay in king/queen-in-Parliament; as with Burke, there could be no challenging the authority of MPs by their constituents between elections.

The most persistent feature of Toryism, undoubtedly, was ongoing identification with Great Britain and its institutions and a parallel suspicion, if not hostility, toward the United States. The run-up to World War I saw insistent Conservative pressure for Canadian financial support for the British navy in its rivalry with Germany. Entry into the so-called Great War was not even a matter of debate in 1914; Canada was at war if Britain was at war. The commitment of blood and treasure during that war was dramatic, involving over 60,000 deaths on the front lines and moving Canada domestically toward a much more organized type of capitalist economy than before. The English–French rift unleashed by conscription in 1917 was a further consequence of the desire to make good on English Canada's commitments to the mother country.

John A. Macdonald had initiated the anti-American tilt in Conservative politics with his "A British subject I was born, a British subject I shall die" stance in his last election campaign of 1891. Something of the same spirit was at work in the 1911 reciprocity election, with the Conservatives defending Canada's economic links to the British empire. The Ottawa Conference of 1932, called at Prime Minister R. B. Bennett's initiative to strengthen imperial preferences at the time of the Depression, was a further example of a pro-British orientation; and something of the same direction carried over into the Diefenbaker government of 1957–63, the last that can be called Tory in this more traditional sense.

However, conservatism has had another face in recent decades. This conservatism is perfectly at home in the glass-and-aluminum towers of corporate Canada; in the quick pace and tempo of North American life; in a market-driven version of public policy. It firmly supports the rollback of the state, deregulation and privatization, cuts in social expenditure, and a fairly instrumentalist approach to culture, education, or scientific research. This version of conservatism is really neoconservatism of the Margaret Thatcher/Ronald Reagan variety. It held sway at the federal level and in many parts of English Canada in the 1980s and still appeals to both Reform and Conservative supporters, witness the recent federal election. Close in spirit to laissez-faire capitalism of a century or two ago, such an ideology sees the freeing up of individual and corporate initiative and the aggregate production of wealth as activities of the highest order. The private is by definition superior to the public, and the individual or the familial is of greater importance than society as a whole.

There is a further aspect to the Reform Party, in particular, that breaks fundamentally with an earlier Toryism. This stems from its populist western roots and its faith in forms of direct democracy such as referenda, initiatives, and recall that would be abhorent to those with Burkean views. As a result, the Reform Party may be more successful in positioning itself as the voice of Canadian conservatism in a democratic era than the Progressive Conservative Party of Brian Mulroney or Kim Campbell.

There is an odd mix of values at work in conservatism of recent vintage. Some of a fundamentalist, "family values" persuasion may be thoroughly neoconservative where market values are concerned, but quite traditional in their opposition to social movements or communities — feminist, gay, ethnic — that violate their received version of English-Canadian society. Others can be fairly liberal on social issues but neoconservative on economic. Still others, although only a minority, may reject neoconservatism in favour of a more community-minded version of conservatism in the first place.

The market-driven version of Canadian conservatism has a distinctly pro-American flavour to it, in sharp contrast to conservatism of the past. Gone is not merely the British connection, but any emphasis on those features of English-Canadian society that might make it somewhat different from the United States. It is not that the adherents of the right do not see themselves as Canadians; there was, however, a strong tendency to identify with the American right, very much in the ascendancy in the United States over the previous decade. Contemporary English-Canadian conservatives are also less given to nationalist reflexes or cultural preoccupations as compared to a hard-nosed reading of economic interests. The latter, in a period of globalization and emerging trade blocs, leads them to support North American and hemispheric free trade, deregulation, tax cuts, et cetera.

Is there a possible blending of such conservatism with more liberal and social democratic elements in English-Canadian political culture? At first blush, the prospects would not appear bright. Many who identify with the latter opposed the Canada–U.S. Free Trade Agreement in 1988 or the North American Free Trade Agreement (NAFTA) less passionately, to be sure, in 1993; many are given to a more nationalist posture regarding the United States in culture or foreign policy; many would oppose the market nostrums of the right as excessively ideological and destructive of other values, for instance, community, social justice, or environmental sustainability.

If we scratch below the surface, we may just possibly find greater cause for optimism. Canadian conservatives are not all of a hard-nosed neoconservative mould; indeed, one can argue that the shift to the right went less far in Canada in the 1980s than it did in Great Britain or the United States, that social expenditures in particular suffered less. Yes, cutbacks were the rule in many jurisdictions; yet a basic commitment to programs like medicare and old age security, even to unemployment insurance and welfare, persisted. Nor was privatization in Canada applied with quite the same frenzy as in Thatcher's Britain. To a degree, the spirit of live and let live may have helped mute ideological rigidity, especially at the federal level; to a degree, Canadian conservatives buy into the welfare state even while preaching the virtues of fiscal restraint; to a degree, they temper their adherence to market ideology with lip service to redistributive programs. Although the Reform Party, if it is to be taken at its word, is less inclined to flexibility in these areas than the Conservative Party has been.

In any English-Canadian nation we can imagine, a conservative element will certainly be present. But the contemporary variant of conservatism, just like the older form, will need to recognize that the price of continuing influence lies in tempering some of the harder edges. This means, for example, a less strident critique of the role of the state than is found on the American right, reflecting the historically different role the state has had to play in a geographically vast but thinly populated country like our own. It means accepting the legitimacy of cultural nationalism in an era of globalization, even while pursuing freer trade and freer markets abroad. It means some balancing off of casino capitalism and entrepreneurial gusto with social responsibility toward the 90 percent or more of the population who will never acquire great wealth, and to the losers in global restructuring, industrial downsizing, and technological change. And for its more fundamentalist adherents, it means recognizing that in a pluralistic and largely secular society, morality, on a whole range of sensitive issues, cannot be legislated, but will be practised by people according to their own inner lights. Is English-Canadian conservatism up to these challenges?

The Liberal Strain

In a number of important respects, English Canada is a liberal society. It has a strong commitment to individual liberty, recently entrenched in the Charter of Rights and Freedoms. It has enjoyed forms of representative government for over two centuries. It has neither set its face against reform nor lived in nostalgic fixation on the past. It is strongly "middle-class" in value and orientation. It has had a capitalist market economy from the beginning. A party calling itself Liberal has for the past century, more often than not, been the governing party in Ottawa and a political force of some importance in the provinces.

What kind of liberalism, however, are we talking about? In the English-Canadian case, we have generally had a nonradical version of liberalism, something that should come as no surprise in light of the absence of a revolutionary tradition in this country (the failed rebellion of 1837 aside). I do not intend here to romanticize the English Civil War of the 1640s, the Glorious Revolution of 1688–89, the American War of Independence, or the tumultuous events of the French Revolution, but we should recognize that periods heralding or accompanying crises or breaks in a country's history are also periods of intense political creativity and radicalization. In other words, some of the great names of political theory — Hobbes, Locke, Montesquieu, Rousseau, Madison, and Jefferson — have been associated with the aforementioned events.

We have lacked such names in Canada, by and large, as Frank Underhill noted many years ago; what we have had instead is a more derivative type of political thought, closely attuned to practical politics and day-to-day concerns. Just as Canadian Toryism was modelled on Great Britain, so Canadian liberalism largely looked to Great Britain and the United States for its models. There is little by way of an *original* Canadian liberal thought (save, perhaps, on the theory and practice of federalism), and little of that reflexive thinking sparked by intense political crisis.

This near vacuum makes it more difficult to pin down Canadian liberalism or to associate it with any one name. Yet just as Burke served as a point of departure for our discussion of Toryism, John Stuart Mill may help us focus our discussion of liberalism.

There are a number of features of Mill's writings of the mid-19th century that I would highlight: a) a belief in individual liberty, especially freedom of thought and expression, as cardinal; b) a belief in representative government with a well-nigh universal franchise as its underpinning; c) a general support for a market economy and for the accompanying principles of private property; d) an opening to forms of governmental intervention where markets fail or basic needs like public education need to be addressed; e) some sensitivity to the interests of the working classes and to questions of equality of opportunity.

Canadian liberals have embraced these features in varying degrees over time. The first three have been there from the beginning, although the nature of the commitment to individual liberty or representative government is somewhat different in the 20th century from the 19th. The fourth and fifth features were to become more important in the aftermath of World War I, the Great Depression, and World War II. It does not follow that Canadian liberalism values each of these equally, or that they coexist in complete harmony with one another. But they all play a part in the story.

Canadian liberals, in general, were less inclined than conservatives to value order as the supreme good. They were heirs to a tradition that had challenged the abuse of authority — be it on the part of the Stuart monarchs, of George III and his government in the Thirteen Colonies, or of the French ancien régime.

Within British North America, there had been a Family Compact, bespeaking power and privilege, linked to the British crown. Those merchants and farmers, lawyers and artisans who felt excluded from the political process were at the centre of the struggle for responsible government. They were also avid believers in freedom of the press — a major arm in the battle against oligarchical power — in freedom of religion, and in freedom of expression generally. William Lyon Mackenzie, "the Great Reformer," breathed the spirit of a crusading liberalism; but in a more moderate form, George Brown with his support for "representation by population," Edward Blake, and others upheld liberal principles.

There would not be any codification of such principles in the British North America Act. In contrast to their American counterparts, Canadian liberals did not press the case for an entrenched Bill of Rights; they would be content, by and large, with the constitutional traditions developed in Great Britain and the protections of the common law.

The Canadian experience with both individual and group rights was far from sterling in the century that followed: the civil liberties of aboriginals, francophone minorities, immigrants, Japanese Canadians, radicals, trade unionists, religious dissenters, and others were violated at various times. In periods of crisis, moreover, such as the two world wars or the October Crisis of 1970, liberties were easily swept aside in the name of order, by Liberal no less than by Conservative governments.

The increased emphasis on rights internationally in the aftermath of World War II, for instance, the Universal Declaration of Human Rights adopted by the United Nations in 1948, coupled with the influence of American practice in these matters, had something to do with an evolution in Canadian attitudes. The first move in the direction of a Bill of Rights is linked to a Conservative prime minister of Tory disposition, John Diefenbaker, in 1960; the second, more substantial, is linked to the name of Pierre Trudeau. The latter had, of course, experienced firsthand the unsavoury practices of Maurice Duplessis in Quebec, although ironically he was also the man whose proclamation of the War Measures Act in 1970 had itself sparked questions about the inviolability of basic rights in this country. Be that as it may, there can be no disputing that the Charter of Rights and Freedoms, adopted at Trudeau's behest in 1981, affirms the basic liberties that Mill, with greater eloquence it is true, had defended in his classic *On Liberty* of 1859. Certainly the charter has become a remarkably important part of the Canadian constitution in the very short period since its adoption and, on the English-Canadian side in particular, testament to deep liberal commitments that cross party lines. One cannot imagine a future English Canada without a Bill of Rights of this kind.

Representative government involved less of a battle in Canada than in Great Britain; there was well-nigh complete agreement between the parties regarding a broad form of suffrage — male-only it is true — well before Confederation. The extension of the franchise to women was to occur with relatively little acrimony at the federal level by 1921. (Although extension of the franchise to female relatives of combatants at the front had been a far more partisan measure in the autumn of 1917!) Status Indians and Inuit, as well as Chinese and Japanese Canadians, were, however, deprived of voting rights for long decades; only in the post-World War II period did Canadian practice catch up with the theory of universal and equal rights to representation. Section 3 of the charter has now entrenched this in our constitution.

There is another aspect of liberal democratic practice, however, that has figured less prominently in Canada. This is the more direct form of democracy associated with referenda, and with participation in decision-making at the local level, in educational institutions, economic institutions, and the like. There are hints at the latter forms of participation in Mill's *Representative Government*, and there is the experience of other polities — Switzerland, Australia, Ireland, various American states — where the former is concerned. Our own use of referenda/plebiscites at the Canada-wide level — Charlottetown in 1992, conscription in 1942, prohibition in 1898 — has been limited; at the provincial level, as well, these have been more the exception than the rule. Nor is there evidence of very widespread popular participation in municipal affairs, school boards, and other community-related activities. Accordingly there is little reason for English Canadians, liberal or not, who take democracy seriously to rest on their laurels.

Canadian liberals have historically bought into the notion of a market economy and the protection of property rights. These were, after all, ideas defended by English liberals like Locke, Smith, and Mill, and by American liberals, as well. Indeed, such have been the links between liberalism in the political arena and property rights in the economic that both defenders and critics of capitalism — Milton Friedman and C. B. Macpherson come to mind — have often associated the two.

There is little in the track record of Canadian liberalism to suggest opposition to capitalism as such. One can point to agrarian-based movements in western Canada attacking the monopolistic and extortionist side of capitalism, for instance, the grain companies, the railways, and the banks, and to a concomitant need for regulation and control. Some of these tendencies would find their way into the policies of Liberal administrations, federal and provincial. Similarly a more social liberalism, modelled on the late 19th-century British variety and addressing problems of urban blight or working-class poverty, would take flight in Canada, as well, finding greater support among liberals than conservatives. But the essence of Canadian liberalism, in contradistinction to socialism, lay in its acceptance of the underlying premises of the capitalist system. Here an unbroken thread runs from George Brown to C. D. Howe and beyond.

Where Canadian liberalism began to waver in its absolute faith in the marketplace is in certain of the same areas where J. S. Mill had permitted himself some doubts. In book 5, chapter 11 of his *Principles of Political Economy*, Mill had provided for a number of exceptions to the principle of noninterference or laissez-faire. These included public education, regulation of conditions of labour, the provision of relief, public works, and cases where private monopolies would otherwise be the rule. Many examples of state activity in Canada prior to World War I fall into these categories.

John Maynard Keynes carried the liberal argument for state intervention further in his writings of the 1920s and 1930s; noting inherent tendencies in capitalism to insufficient demand and market failure, he advocated the use of government fiscal policy — deficits in periods of high unemployment and low demand, surpluses in periods of economic prosperity — as a remedy.

Canadian liberals were quick to embrace the Keynesian faith in the 1930s and 1940s; indeed, the White Paper on Employment and Income, drafted by the Ministry of Finance in Ottawa in the spring of 1945, represents by all accounts the first public endorsement of Keynesian economics by any Western government. The experience of the Great Depression had tempered the faith of many Canadian liberals in any inherent tendency in capitalism, domestic and international, to equilibrium at high levels of employment. It had also made them more conscious of the importance of distributive questions, both for reasons of social justice and of electoral appeal.

The result was a slow but calculated embrace of the welfare state. Key breakthroughs in this area — old age pensions, unemployment insurance, family allowances, medicare, the Canada Pension Plan — are associated with Liberal administrations over a period of 40 years; such administrations were also prone to introduce changes in labour law that gave trade unions a measure of recognition. From Mackenzie King's Industrial Disputes Investigation Act of 1907 to provisions for government-supervised certification of trade unions in 1944 to the extension of bargaining rights to workers in the public sector in the 1960s, Canadian liberalism has shown some openness in this regard.

How easily can one reconcile the side of liberalism associated with social expenditures or labour reforms with the liberal commitment to the capitalist system as such? Much as Mill, in his later years, wrestled with problems of fairness and equity in the workings of a capitalist system in which he believed, so Canadian liberals have attempted to balance off concerns for entrepreneurial initiative and competitive advantage with concerns for social fairness and a larger public good. At times, they have come closer to the social democratic pole; at others, they have come down a good deal closer to the conservative — or should one not call it market liberal? — one. The temper of English-Canadian society in matters of social and economic policy has often reflected this balance within liberalism itself.

There are a number of other areas where Canadian liberalism mirrors important currents within English-Canadian society. For example, liberalism from the beginning has had a more North American tropism to it than the British tropism associated with conservatism. So much so that, for the first century of Canada's existence, there is something to the argument that would define the conservative version of English Canada as pro-British and anti-American and the liberal version as the reverse. And even today, when there has been an about-turn in liberal versus conservative attitudes toward the United States, as the free trade debate showed, in matters of rights and individual liberty, American liberalism has had a persistent influence on the English-Canadian variety.

Historically Canadian liberalism has shown greater sensitivity to the English–French duality than conservatism. This understanding may reflect the presence of a significant French-Canadian element within the Liberal Party over time. It may also reflect a greater sensitivity to federalism and its workings; a shifting balance between centre and provinces seems to go well with underlying liberal notions of balance and/or separation of powers. How well this experience might serve English-Canadian liberals as regards future changes in the relationship with Quebec or with aboriginal peoples remains to be seen. Here, there is potential conflict between commitment to an unhyphenated notion of individual rights à la the Charter of Rights and Freedoms and to that of group recognition; between the current federal system with its formal equality of the provinces and the quite different set of arrangements that a restructured Canada–Quebec–aboriginal union might entail. The fault lines within English Canada in these matters may well run through Canadian liberalism itself.

Finally multiculturalism is still one more area where, in the post-World War II period, liberals have proven themselves more reflective of deeper currents in English-Canadian society than those to the right of them. In important ways, therefore, English-Canadian society is liberal; but the political culture of English Canada builds on a broader gamut of opinion.

The Social Democratic Strain

A majority of English Canadians do not, and are unlikely to, identify themselves as social democrats. Unlike the conservative and liberal strains, the social democratic one emerged in our own century. In tracing its origins, one can point to a combination of working-class radicalism, agrarian populism, the social gospel tradition within certain Protestant denominations, and university-based intellectuals.

Despite the existence of a social democratic party at the federal level since the 1930s, first the CCF then the NDP, it has never broken through the barrier of third-party status or a 20 percent share of the popular vote. There have been social democratic governments at the provincial level — Saskatchewan most of all, Manitoba, British

Columbia, and Ontario. Nonetheless, social democracy in English Canada is a distinctly minority tradition, in contrast to what has been the case in a good number of European societies, or even in Australia or New Zealand. And the disastrous showing by the NDP in the 1993 federal election raises doubts about its future place.

Why then highlight social democracy at all in this discussion? What are its unique theoretical and practical appeals? How does it interact with both liberal and conservative strains within the larger English-Canadian political culture?

The tendency in most accounts of the CCF/NDP tradition is to emphasize the influence of the British Labour and Fabian tradition. This is both historically and factually accurate, insofar as a good number of trade union leaders who saw themselves as socialists in early 20th-century Canada were themselves of British origins, and a certain number of the intellectuals who coauthored the Regina Manifesto of 1933 or the mid-1930s volume *Social Planning for Canada* had themselves attended British universities. There were other sources for left-of-centre radicalism: syndicalism, populism, Marxism. Still, Labour-style social democracy proved the most enduring.

In looking for a figure comparable to Burke or Mill to ground this discussion, I am tempted, however, to reach outside the British socialist tradition. The name that comes to mind is that of Jean-Jacques Rousseau, someone who was neither British nor a social democrat, as we tend to understand the term today.

A number of elements in Rousseau's political writings are relevant to our theme: a) a belief in the basic goodness of human beings; b) a notion of equality whereby every citizen has something and no one has too much; c) the concept of a general will superior to the sum of the particular wills of the individual members of society; d) a belief that democracy entails some direct participation by citizens in the affairs of their community/society. Let us see how much of this finds expression within English-Canadian social democracy.

It may sound terribly naive to speak about human nature in such Manichaean terms as good and evil. Nonetheless, a major difference between a social democratic and a more conservative or even liberal view may well revolve around this question. Social democrats do not see humans as egotistical and power-seeking in the way that many to the right of them do; or to put it another way, they do not see in such impulses a sufficient or satisfactory basis for understanding the functioning of society.

There is, social democrats invoking the spirit of Rousseau might claim, a legitimate sphere of love of self for human beings; but there is also a capacity to feel for one's fellow humans which, translated into political terms, leads to a desire to develop social arrangements that mitigate suffering and seek to maximize the conditions for human development. We cannot assume that there is an invisible social hand that will miraculously bring about societal good, much as laissez-faire liberals believe in an invisible economic hand. Nor can we assume that social conflicts, and international ones, as well, are the inevitable lot of human beings. Given appropriate social and economic conditions, humans are capable of a good deal of harmonious, even virtuous behaviour.

This view of human nature colours a second feature of social democratic thinking — its view of equality. For conservatives, and a good many liberals, as well, people are unequal almost by definition, having different genetic characteristics and predispositions, being born into different social backgrounds, bringing different degrees of intelligence and entrepreneurship to their activities. The unequal distribution of wealth and property characteristic of capitalist societies is a fair reflection of these inherent inequalities. At most, a modest degree of redistribution through the tax system and social spending may be justified to prevent the poorest from falling through the cracks.

Social democrats are closer to the Rousseauean faith in natural equality. They do not accept the premise that the existing distribution of wealth is just or natural, and that physical or mental differences in capacity between different individuals justifies the degree of inequality in living conditions, economic power, and political power that goes with it. They do believe that a certain levelling of wealth within societies, across societies (that is, internationally), and across the generations, for instance, through an inheritance tax, would make for a more just, and ultimately more democratic, social order.

Everything, of course, is relative; hence English-Canadian social democrats have never subscribed to a notion of absolute equality; nor did they advocate that total socialization of the means of production associated with 20th-century Marxist-Leninist regimes. In their more radical phase, say, the 1930s, they may have called for public ownership of finance and of key manufacturing and resource industries and for a measure of centralized economic planning. In their more moderate post-World War II incarnation, they largely abandoned their faith in these two tenets, arguing instead for a fairer distribution of wealth through social expenditures and limited forms of public ownership.

Even these demands in recent years have met with growing resistance on two grounds: a) dissatisfaction with the scope and scale of the welfare state and with its accompanying levels of taxation; b) dissatisfaction with the performance of certain public enterprises and with their responsiveness to community needs. This dissatisfaction has had significant implications for what NDP governments, when they have come to power in recent years, have been able to undertake. Yet the aspiration to greater equality of condition, both domestically and internationally, remains at the heart of the social democratic credo. And social democracy can take some of the credit for the historical moves toward the welfare state and toward a more interventionist role for government in Canada.

Social measures, however, have seldom been introduced into Canada in the name of socialism, not even by NDP governments. Rather, the appeal has been to the notion of community. One thinks of agrarian communities in western Canada in the first part of this century, where the cooperative movement took hold. One thinks of the trade union movement, couching its broader appeal to community, as opposed to corporate, interests. One thinks also of the articulation of a sense of national community by CCF intellectuals such as Graham Spry, F. R. Scott, and others. Not only was there a concern for Canadian independence vis-à-vis *both* Britain and the United States — a rare note in the interwar period — there was also concern for the cultural and social bases of citizenship and for a strong federal government that could bind Canadians together.

In general, left-of-centre English Canadians think of Canada in terms of community; they place less emphasis on the purely individual dimensions of citzenship than do liberals; they are more open to notions of group rights; and they tend to believe in a national whole that is more than the sum of its individual parts. It would be unfair to equate this, in unmediated fashion, with Rousseau's notion of the general will, but social democrats are more inclined to Rousseauean ideas of community than are their liberal or conservative counterparts.

What about the participatory or direct notions of democracy to be found in Rousseau? Here, the social democratic legacy is distinctly more uneven. On the one hand, both the CCF and the NDP and its leaders have from the beginning bought into a notion of parliamentary sovereignty, rejecting thereby any broad application of direct democracy grounded in notions of popular sovereignty. Yet there was also a strong grass-roots tradition within Canadian social democracy, especially in western Canada, supportive of ideas like popular initiative, recall, and referenda. (Here, there is an interesting overlap with more right-wing forms of populism associated with Social Credit in the 1930s or the Reform Party today.) There are traditions of direct action associated with the trade union movement. And over the past 25 years, the impact of movements like the student left, women, peace, or the environment has been telling. The result is an opening on the left of the Canadian political spectrum to participatory notions of citizenship.

The larger question of the impact of social democracy, both on its political rivals and on English-Canadian political culture, remains. Here one needs to be careful. On the one hand, the social democratic tradition does constitute a striking difference when we compare English Canada with the United States. Along with the greater strength of the trade union movement in post-World War II Canada, it helps explain the more developed nature of our welfare state or a greater openness to public enterprise.

On the other hand, ours is a less developed welfare state than in Scandinavia and parts of Western Europe; our political economy, all said and done, is far more similar (and integrated) to the American than to any other; and our model of society/civilization far more North American than anything else. Just as Tories represented something of an Old World intrusion into a New World society in the 19th century, so social democracy, English-Canadian style, represented something exotic, if not totally foreign, in 20th-century Canada. It could never overcome the obstacle posed by the absence of a social democratic tradition in the United States, or for that matter, the barriers that existed to social democracy in pre-Quiet Revolution Quebec. It could gain a foothold in English Canada, even secure the occasional provincial beachhead; it could not remake English Canada in its own image.

Nor do I see social democracy by itself being able to play such a role in the future. Social democracy's aspirations must be more modest. It has helped make legitimate in Canada social policies like medicare that might not have been introduced otherwise. It has helped soften the purely capitalist features of Canadian society by articulating the case for a counterbalancing and redistributive role for the state. It has helped articulate the needs of social classes and groups, beginning with labour but extending to a whole variety of social movements, that might otherwise have had little voice. It has helped make Canada a more temperate, slightly more just, and certainly more community-minded society than otherwise.

In exchange, however, social democracy has had to make peace with its ideological adversaries. It has had to accept the logic of markets and fiscal discipline and discard an earlier faith in large-scale public ownership and economic planning. It has accepted the basically liberal notion of rights, as entrenched in the Charter of Rights and Freedoms, albeit with somewhat greater openness to the notion of group rights. It has bought a good deal of the king/queen-in-Parliament notion of sovereignty rooted in Toryism and conservatism, although it needs to temper this with elements of the democratic credo rooted in Western populism. The price of acceptability in English Canada has come through discarding a good deal from its own past, while coming to terms with competing political traditions. Does social democracy, if it is to maintain its toehold in English-Canadian political culture, have any choice but to continue to do the same into the future?

5

English Canada and the Larger English-speaking World

C ONSERVATISM, LIBERALISM, AND SOCIAL DEMOCRACY have together helped shape English-Canadian political culture. There is, however, nothing uniquely Canadian or
English-Canadian about these three, for we find their counterparts
in many Western societies. At most, the particular blend — an early
dose of Toryism, a dominant liberal strand, a minority social democratic tradition, shades of populism — gives English Canada its
particular character.

National culture, however, is not one and the same thing as
political ideology or credo. And although there is a conservative,
liberal, and social democratic vision of English Canada, these may
not by themselves, or even in conjunction, resolve foundational
questions about what English Canada is.

Central to English-Canadian identity, it was argued in chapter 3,
is language. Yet from this flows a profound ambiguity. English
Canada must share the language in question with Great Britain,
Ireland, the United States, Australia, New Zealand, South Africa, the
West Indies, and many others. In what sense, then, can language be
a factor constitutive of national identity, particularly when it is one
as universal as English?

This query may seem odd. There are other languages that cross
international boundaries — Spanish, German, and French for starters.

Is there any doubt that Swiss Germans and Germans are not one and the same people? French Swiss and French? Mexicans and Spaniards? Why should nationalities have to have unique languages of their own in order to qualify as distinct? Having earlier determined that nation and state are not one and the same thing, should we now get bogged down in advancing spurious claims about language and nation?

At one level, it is true that things are simpler and more straightforward when languages do not need to be shared. The Japaneseness of Japan has something to do with the fact that no other society uses that language; the same can be said of Farsi and Iran, of Hebrew and Israel, Hungarian and Hungary, Swedish and Sweden, et cetera. In analogous fashion, the claims of aboriginal and tribal peoples throughout the world to national status and identity hinges on the indigenous language its members speak (or once spoke).

However, the sharing of a language does not somehow vitiate national identity; Americans and Australians, for example, are not Britons manqué, nor must they envy the Japanese and the Swedes their linguistic status. There are advantages to being part of language communities that transcend the nation-state; there is more than language to colour national sentiment; and even shared languages take on vocabularies, accents, and dictions of their own, as a cursory familiarity with the different branches of the English, French, German, or Spanish-speaking worlds would suggest.

Of course, there are problems associated with membership in these broad linguistic groupings. It took a while for Americans to assert their unique identity (and version of English) vis-à-vis the onetime mother country; and it is only in this century that American English, reflecting the rise of the United States to world power status, definitively displaced British English as the leading version. As for smaller linguistic communities — the Austrians, the Walloons or Québécois, the Chileans — these may well have inferiority complexes with regard to larger, dominant ones. How easily local dialects and idioms can be dismissed as "provincial" and second-rate by sophisticates of the same language grouping! How much more difficult it may prove for artists and intellectuals, scientists and inventors, entrepreneurs and political figures to win recognition in the metropoles — the purveyors of cultural fashion, economic success, and political sagacity.

Part of the malaise of English-Canadian identity hinges around a similar set of problems. There could be no gainsaying the custodial claims of Britain over English language and culture in the 18th and 19th centuries. Key publishing houses, quarterlies, newspapers, major theatres, leading clubs, and universities were in Britain; the principal financial institutions were headquartered there; the prestige and symbolism of an empire on which the sun never set were associated with the British monarchy and leading families of the realm, with the Colonial Office and the Admiralty, with Whitehall and Westminster. The colonists of British North America were but rubes by comparison. Their railway securities were a safe enough investment; their empty lands and nascent cities safe havens for remittance men and the surplus population of Britain's working-class slums; their political leaders acceptable ornaments on imperial occasions and fit visitors to stately homes. With time, no doubt, Canadian colonials would make their contribution to the larger interests of the empire and redeem the faith the mother country had shown in them; until then, a hefty note of condescension would permeate the British attitude toward those offshoots of English language and culture that bore the names of colony or dominion.

Not all English-speaking Canadians, even at the time of Confederation, lived in the shadow of British approbation (or scorn). The fledgling Canada First Movement of the early years was one attempt to strike out on an uncharted path of national identity; a good deal of subsequent cultural expression, from popular magazines of the late 19th century, to school and university curricula, to the paintings of the Group of Seven, reflected the quite unique characteristics of a new land. Canadian-spoken English, moreover, bore much greater similarity to American diction than to British; and something of the aboriginal, French, and immigrant experience would also mark it. Still, the British connection would both influence and somewhat thwart attempts at forging an English-Canadian identity into the 20th century.

To the degree that this began to change, say in the period between 1918 and 1945, it reflected the declining importance to Canada of

Britain, politically and economically, and the growing importance of the United States. There is little need to emphasize the shift in sources of investment, for instance, in manufacturing and resources, to south of the border; the reorientation of trade relations; or the fact that militarily the American connection, as World War II was to show, was becoming more vital to Canadian security than the British.

The technological spillover was overwhelming — automobiles, airplanes, heavy machinery, consumer products, highway grids and housing designs; the cultural fallout — radio, film, magazine, music, the arts, and the sciences — was scarcely smaller. If there had ever been any doubt about the essential North Americanness of English Canada, these had certainly vanished by the end of World War II. From that point on, the dilemma of English-Canadian identity had clearly become that of differentiating itself from the United States.

While there had been an ocean separating Canada from Britain and inevitable differences between a New World society and an old, Canada had no such obvious barriers with which to defend itself from the United States. Its very geographical proximity reinforced patterns of economic integration; military alliances and political partnership in the Cold War period cemented a sense of common interest, a few dissenting voices notwithstanding; cultural domination was the inevitable by-product of an American population base 12 times that of English Canada and of a society fully realizing its manifest destiny. Britain itself seemed for a time but a province of a larger English-speaking universe, which the United States bestrode; what more could English Canada aspire to than junior league status?

Canadian entertainers who wanted to make it could only do so in the United States; Canadian academics worth their salt would hope to publish or lecture south of the border; research and development in Canada was like a sideshow to the formidable American effort; Canadian TV shows would have to compete against far better financed and more slickly produced American programming; the Canadian film industry, for years, would have to be content with the documentary crumbs that Hollywood had left it.

At the rear window of the American empire, English Canadians had no clear voice of their own. They had all the material comforts that flowed from continental integration and an access to American culture unfiltered by language or space. They could be just like Americans for most purposes, although if pressed to highlight the differences, where international organizations or the outside world were concerned, they would define themselves as a slightly less brash version of English-speaking North American. Within the English-speaking world, they might ply the Commonwealth connection, their middle power status, or their less drawled and masticated rendition of Shakespeare's tongue. Still, there was something a bit pathetic about English Canada's attempts to convince itself and others of its own identity.

There was one serious attempt to sound the alarm — the Report of the Royal Commission on the Arts, Letters, and Sciences of 1951. This study underlined the degree of English-Canadian cultural dependence on the United States; it called for federal spending on postsecondary education, scientific research, and the arts; and it helped set the stage for the creation of the Canada Council in 1957. Yet government spending or no government spending, the short-term prognosis for English Canada and its culture did not look rosy.

Did things suddenly take a change for the better from the 1960s on? It is hard to say for certain. But the wave of English-Canadian nationalism that hit during that period — the critique of American policy in Vietnam, of American domination over the Canadian economy, trade union movement, magazines, publishing, university curricula, and much besides — struck a responsive chord. And it coincided with a number of changes internally — the deepening of the welfare state, the extension of the postsecondary educational system, the celebration of Canada's centennial and Expo 67, the emergence of a new generation of English-Canadian novelists and playwrights, artists and filmmakers less interested in making it in the United States than in addressing the Canadian experience on its own terms. These new currents found a receptive audience across the country and seemed to herald a maturing of English-Canadian identity.

Or so it might have seemed by comparison with the 1940s or 1950s. In fact, the hard challenge of coexisting side by side with the United States did not suddenly disappear; nor did the integrating currents that had so dominated Canadian life through the early postwar decades suddenly give way to full-sprung independence. The 1980s were to see the pressures for ever closer alignment with the United States, in the economic arena in particular, resume with a vengeance.

The 1960s, nonetheless, represented a new beginning. For a little like the Quiet Revolution in Quebec (if I may be permitted the comparison), the decade marked the birth of a peculiarly English-Canadian sensibility. A sensibility that was certainly not British, but no less decidedly not American; one that was perfectly at home with its language and its status as one of the English-speaking communities of the world; one that looked to its own history, geography, and development as a society for the hallmarks of its identity; one, finally, that much like Quebec nationalism, was dependent on a good deal of state support to help get it off the ground.

There was a bit of bravura, even *prepotenza,* in the air as English-Canadian nationalists of one stripe or another set about the task of charting their brave new society of the future. But compared to the diffidence of old or the branch-plant mentality that had held sway for so much of the postwar period, the decade held forth a promise of renewal.

Some of this potential may well have been fulfilled; some of it was to come to naught. But one lasting legacy as we cast about in search of English Canada three decades later may be a newfound sense of cultural mooring. The self-definition of English Canada ceases to be problematic the less it is based on purely negative imagery. It was not enough, for example, to decry British influences in the past only to succumb to American; nor would it be enough to denounce American as some great evil in itself. Instead, a positive sense of English-Canadian identity will have to be based on what is authentically English-Canadian — however much or little this may overlap or even draw on the experience of the larger English-speaking countries. The standard for excellence and acclaim could not be driven by what might or might not prevail in London or New York — not that we should turn our backs on these venues. Rather, English-Canadian culture would need to reflect the lived experiences of urban and rural English Canada, its manifold communities, regions, and cultures, their long-suppressed or unexpressed aspirations, their successes and failures at cohabitation in a harsh and difficult climate. And through these experiences it would ultimately capture a more universal idiom.

So perhaps here is where we see the English-Canadian point of entry to the larger English-speaking universe. It is not as a sidekick to empires — British or American as the case may be. Nor is it through a politics of resentment, strident in its grievance against larger forces beyond its control. Neither imperial power nor victim, English Canada is slowly taking its place in the middle tier of English-speaking nations. Its voice must reflect the cultural creativity of recent decades, the quiet confidence that comes from finally discovering who you are. And that, as the remainder of this book will try to show, requires a sense both of the others with whom we share a country and of the plurality of forces upon which English Canada itself rests.

6

The Aboriginal Component

THE SUBJECT OF ABORIGINALS is one of the more difficult topics for Canadians at the end of the 20th century to address. Even as I write these lines, the newspapers are full of accounts of substance abuse among the Innu people of Davis Inlet, Labrador. Suicide rates, incidence of disease, and poverty levels are far greater among aboriginal communities across the country than among the nonaboriginal population. The history of residential schools is a dismal one; the exclusion of aboriginal peoples from the political, economic, and social life of mainstream Canada an unsung and troubling part of our past.

In a broader context, contact between European and indigenous peoples in the New World, as debate provoked by the quinticentenary of Columbus's voyages suggested, turned out tragically for the latter. Whole civilizations were destroyed and populations decimated; traditional modes of life became impossible; pre-Christian religions and cultures uprooted; land and resources alienated. Whether the colonists were Spanish or Portuguese, French or British, the story seems to have been the same. Aboriginal peoples became dispossessed and powerless in the lands of their ancestors, subjects and dependents to the new masters who came to call these spaces their own.

There is no need to romanticize precontact civilizations (for instance, wars of conquest and enslavement were not uncommon among them), to acknowledge the wanton destruction that European settlement entailed. Nor is it a matter of singling out New World indigenous peoples as the sole victims of outside military conquest, even genocide. The annals of history — Asian, African, Near Eastern, European — are filled with similar bloodstained accounts.

The fact remains, however, that conquest lies at the origin of the settlement of the New World. Technologically and militarily advanced civilizations were able to impose their will on less developed ones; white, Christian, and European civilizations on nonwhite, non-Christian, non-European. New World lands were not the empty wastes of which John Locke had written in his *Second Treatise on Government;* nor were its peoples the primitive savages without laws, kings, or religion that various Europeans had disdainfully decried. They were, however, an "other," whom settlers and creoles throughout the Americas would overrun.

Some would use treaties, some the sword alone; some would fight wars of extermination, clearing the pampas and temperate lands for their own use; others would leave bits and pieces of rocky soil, or jungle, or postage-stamp reserves for the survivors of their own expanding needs. The upshot in all cases was but a shadowy existence for the hemisphere's first peoples, caught between a vanishing world and one alien to their being.

State structures — bureaucratic, military, legalistic to the core — became the norm; land came to be divided up and appropriated into individual plots; money was the all-powerful agent of exchange; railways and ports, grain elevators and mining camps, cities and frontier towns the harbingers of a new economic age. Proselytizing religions, intolerant of what had come before, intransigent in their symbols, provided the cultural and ideological underpinnings for what ensued.

There would be little space for indigenous customs and institutions in this brave new world. Capitalism — Anglo-Saxon or Latin — would put paid to group and collective forms of ownership common to most aboriginal societies. European notions of sovereignty, developed in an age of absolutism and the emerging nation-state, would be taken over into the Americas and incorporated into the postcolonial states; even democratic formulations, like those associated with the American Revolution, did not extend the notion of citizenship and entitlement to aboriginal peoples. These were less the subjects than the objects of politics in New World societies, having no rights of their own. Their cultural practices and ceremonies were suppressed or rendered insignificant. Shorn of their identities, aboriginal peoples came to occupy the bottom rungs of the social scale.

In one fashion or another, many did survive. In the Canadian case, for example, reserves provided a real, if barely sustainable basis, for aboriginal communities, especially when removed from larger urban centres; in more northern regions, where whites were few and far between, traditional forms of hunting, trapping, and fishing could be sustained somewhat longer. Missionaries and their schools, for all their well-documented cultural downside, did provide aboriginals with some of the skills required in mainstream white society. And in the urban areas, where increasing numbers of aboriginal people sought their fortune if for no other than economic reasons, there were a few successes alongside the dismal, skid-row failures.

Yet the overall story of aboriginal peoples in this country is not a happy one. Despite the not insignificant sums of money the Department of Indian Affairs has been spending in recent decades, there is little evidence of any wholesale improvement in the living conditions of many aboriginal communities. Despite a more articulate, university-educated aboriginal leadership that has arisen recently, there is much at the grass-roots level in both urban and nonurban aboriginal communities that is not being addressed. And despite a more favourable attitude toward aboriginal people among non-aboriginal Canadians in recent years, and a sense of responsibility for some of the sins of the past, we are still years away from rectifying the damage or laying the foundations of a relationship based upon equity and trust.

So where, spurning sentimentality on the one hand and hollow gestures on the other, do we turn? I, for one, am not at all uncomfortable with the idea of aboriginal self-government that was abroad in the run-up to the Charlottetown Accord; in a more general sense, I am open to some significant transfer of economic resources to aboriginal peoples as part of a comprehensive recognition of their distinct, national status within Canada. But hard thinking about the trade-offs between enhanced aboriginal status, collectively speaking, and the present status of aboriginals as individual citizens, however marginalized, of Canada is required. And difficult questions about the future relationship between aboriginal and nonaboriginal governments cannot be brushed aside.

We cannot undo centuries of uneven history, political and economic relations, and forced socialization with the wave of a hand. Nor is there much point in Canadians of the present generation engaging in acts of contrition and guilt for the deeds of those who came before; pushed to its limits, this would be dysfunctional, even suicidal, undermining the legitimacy of our own claims to citizenship in this land. There is something more practical that is required — recognition by nonaboriginals of the distinctive history and character of Canada's first peoples. For these peoples did not migrate to these shores in the past century or two, as most of English Canada's inhabitants did; nor is their relationship to the political structures we have erected or the economic and social arrangements we have developed the same as that of other groups.

In a sense, aboriginal people constitute involuntary citizens of Canada. They were never asked their opinions on the French or British regimes, nor on Confederation and what ensued. Disenfranchised for almost a century, they had little choice but to accept the weight of laws and dominant economic interests, and to endure in what lands they had been left. Their cultural identities, for most purposes, were denied, and their maladaptation to mainstream Canadian society became a palpable reality from the start.

To recognize this denial, even at this late date, is to acknowledge that aboriginal peoples have reasons to spurn assimilation and to seek, within the limits of the possible, alternative solutions. Two options, however, need to be ruled out from the start. First, there can be no going back to the status quo ante, some earlier stage of civilization and social organization that existed before the Europeans arrived. Technology cannot be uninvented, English unlearned, Christianity extirpated, liberal democratic precepts cast aside, regardless of attempts to revive traditional notions of spirituality, to give a new lease of life to native languages, to allow aboriginals to touch base where possible with older tribal customs. Second, aboriginal peoples, few in numbers, divided up into multiple tribal groupings, scattered across the length and breadth of the country, cannot aspire to something as heady as nation-state status. What would the boundaries of such an entity include? What degree of political and cultural coherence might it have? What would be the basis for its economic livelihood? What means of military self-defence would it have? What would be the citizenship rights of aboriginals living outside of its territory? What about nonaboriginals within its borders? A whole series of questions would come with sovereignty as the term is used in international affairs, stirring enormous conflict.

Rather, self-affirmation seems to lie in achieving forms of aboriginal self-government that stop short of sovereignty and that entail ongoing association with nonaboriginal Canadian society. To invoke the distinction made in chapter 1, it lies in recognizing aboriginal nations, as opposed to aboriginal nation-states. What concrete form might such recognition take?

The most compelling would seem to be on a territorial basis, using existing reservations or historical patterns of settlement. Yet immediately, ticklish problems of balancing off aboriginal and nonaboriginal interests arise. Clearly not all of the unassigned territory of Ontario, Alberta, or British Columbia is to be recognized as aboriginal land! Perhaps five percent, perhaps ten percent may come to be so designated once negotiations have been carried out. Compensation would have to be provided to nonaboriginals for the loss of access to such lands and resources that they currently enjoy. Ownership of aboriginal lands would presumably come to be vested in aboriginal nations as a whole, with guarantees that the fruits of such ownership and related economic activities benefit all their members. Mechanisms for coordinating economic resources and certain governmental activities among aboriginal nations may have to be devised, while procedures for coordinating land use and other policies between aboriginal and nonaboriginal governments would have to be put in place.

It would be unacceptable, for example, to have a series of environmental safeguards operating at the level of a province but not within aboriginal lands; fisheries regulations cannot be neatly separated into aboriginal and nonaboriginal compartments; and one cannot imagine vastly different criminal and civil legal systems operating between them. Moreover, the standard of services available to aboriginal people on aboriginal lands would need, with time, to match reasonably closely the standards prevalent in nonaboriginal society, if aboriginal self-government is to garner the support of aboriginal peoples.

The business of establishing a working model for aboriginal self-government, therefore, is no easy matter. Nor is it the case that what may work in Nunavut or in largely aboriginal-populated areas north of the 54th parallel would work closer to areas of major nonaboriginal settlement. The economic viability of self-governing aboriginal communities, moreover, would depend directly on the types of resources with which they were endowed, and on the aptitude of aboriginal self-governments to manage these effectively. For the quid pro quo for the transfer of lands and resources by provincial or federal governments to aboriginal ones would almost certainly be the reduction and progressive elimination of services to such communities paid for by nonaboriginal Canadians. With their new powers, aboriginal governments would thus acquire the responsibility for raising revenue and providing the bulk of services on aboriginal land. They would need to be largely self-reliant, and fully accountable to their constituents.

It is not my intention to enter into a discussion of the many details aboriginal self-government would entail. This can be left for royal commissions, experts and, most of all, the aboriginal peoples themselves to grapple with. But there are at least two other issues that require comment.

The first is the status of aboriginal peoples living outside reserves or what may in future be designated as aboriginal lands. It is very difficult to conceive of aboriginal self-government operating under such circumstances; at most, it may be possible to provide special services — for instance, educational, health, community — to aboriginal people in larger centres, with some provisions for grass-roots input and control. Self-government, with its implications of full-scale autonomy and parallel institutional structures, is an impossibility for aboriginal peoples in the context of diverse, integrated urban centres. It would create an administrative nightmare of the first order, sowing the seeds of endless contention between aboriginal minorities and the much larger nonaboriginal population. Aboriginal Canadians wishing to live under governments of their own control will have to do so where they constitute the majority or the whole of the population, primarily on aboriginal lands.

A second issue, larger in scope, regards the mesh between aboriginal self-government and the overall political governance of Canada. Since we are not talking about aboriginal nation-states, it follows that aboriginals will continue to be citizens of Canada. What sort of inputs should aboriginals, living on self-governing lands, have into the political affairs of province or federal government?

To the degree that aboriginal nations do not come to exercise certain powers — for example, with regard to external affairs, defence, trade and commerce federally, or environmental regulations, postsecondary institutions, major highways, and ferries provincially — there is no reason their members should not have the same rights to elect representatives to legislatures or Parliament as do other Canadians. Yet to the degree that aboriginal nations will be self-governing, it seems unreasonable to give them any voice in determining policies that would essentially apply to nonaboriginal Canadians. There is, therefore, a dilemma regarding aboriginal representation.

One possible way around this problem is to make provision for separate representation by aboriginal nations in legislatures and Parliament. Aboriginal people living on aboriginal lands would elect these at the same time as the nonaboriginal population (and aboriginals living outside aboriginal lands) chose theirs. Aboriginal representatives so designated would have voting rights in matters where aboriginal nations were subject to provincial or federal jurisdiction; they would have no such rights where aboriginal governments were, in fact, autonomous. There might still remain a series of grey areas that would need clarification; but a delineation along the lines sketched above would provide the basis for aboriginal representation in provincial and federal arenas, while recognizing their distinctive character as largely self-governing nations.

Some such modality becomes all the more important when we start thinking through the synchronization of aboriginal and nonaboriginal governance. Where laws and regulations are to be general in application, it is best to provide for direct aboriginal representation at the provincial and federal level; otherwise, aboriginal nations will find their governments bogged down in endless negotiations, doing little more than interfacing with provincial and federal departments or agencies. From the nonaboriginal point of view, as well, the presence of aboriginal representatives in legislatures and Parliament will serve two useful purposes: 1) it will remind nonaboriginals of aboriginal concerns on a whole range of issues up for discussion; 2) it will reassure nonaboriginal Canadians that in recognizing aboriginal governments they are not simply establishing territorial enclaves with long-term aspirations to sovereignty. Aboriginal representatives in legislatures and Parliament would help provide an important counterweight to any pretensions by various aboriginal governments to be the sole voices of their peoples. Checks and balances may serve aboriginal peoples in good stead, just as they serve nonaboriginal ones.

One final point remains. This discussion has been primarily concerned with the question of aboriginal identity and with some of the issues that aboriginal self-government might pose. What requires underlining where English-Canadian identity is concerned is something slightly different. There is an aboriginal dimension to the history, geography, and culture of this country that we ignore at our peril. To treat this as something extraneous is to cut us off from the living roots of the Canadian *imaginaire*, from peoples who, more than any other, have had this country and its habitat as their home. This is not a matter of seeking to appropriate aboriginal identity as our own, but quite the contrary — it is a matter of acknowledging the legitimacy of a distinct aboriginal identity and of the need to work out a new political relationship between aboriginals and non-aboriginals that takes it into account. To the degree that we succeed in achieving this goal, we simultaneously help lay the foundations for a pluralistic and open English Canada at peace with itself and its better political traditions.

7

Multiculturalism and
Its Limits

AS WAS NOTED EARLIER, the term *English Canada* sets off alarm bells where ethnic and cultural communities are concerned. Any implication that Canadians of British origin have superior rights and status when compared to the equal or larger number of Canadians of non-British background is certain to arouse resentment. Any modification of the name *Canada* with the adjective *English* may be interpreted by some as a legitimization of the linguistic and cultural attributes of one particular group.

Over the past three decades, as the Canada–Quebec debate has unfolded, "third force" Canadians as they used to be called, that is, the members of our diverse ethnic communities, have increasingly made their voices heard. They resisted any definition of Canada by the Royal Commission on Bilingualism and Biculturalism of the 1960s as a purely bicultural society, imposing the term *multicultural* in its place; they argued stridently against any consecration of the notion of "founding peoples" in our constitutional texts; and they invoked Charter of Rights and Freedoms provisions such as sections 15 and 27 in insisting on the fundamental equality that must prevail in the treatment of all Canadians, irrespective of ethnic origin and background.

The emergence of multiculturalism as a force in Canadian politics was a belated response to a sociological transformation going back to the turn of the century. Waves of immigration pouring into Canada at that period from Central, Eastern, and southern Europe could not but, with time, dilute the overwhelmingly Anglo-Saxon character of Canada outside Quebec. The further migration of millions to this country in the post-World War II period and the removal of de facto barriers to non-European migration in the 1960s would deeply alter the face of Canada and its urban centres in particular. Visible minorities, from the West Indies, Central and South America, the Far East, the Indian subcontinent, the Middle East, even Africa, have taken on a new importance, to a point where they will constitute 15 percent of the total population of Canada by the year 2000. Audible minorities, speaking over 100 different languages and mirroring a myriad of cultures, have become an integral part of the Canadian mosaic. To deny their specificity and their presence is to play ostrich, redneck, or worse.

At the same time, people of diverse backgrounds have chosen to migrate to Canada and, in most cases, to become Canadian citizens. This decision means that they and their offspring subscribe to the political, legal, and other features that characterize this country and cannot expect special treatment or recognition as groups apart. Nor can they simply import with them blood feuds and hatreds from countries from which they originate and give them new expression on Canadian soil. The price of forging a new nationality out of diverse elements is a fair degree of tolerance and goodwill all around.

What, then, does multiculturalism represent when it comes to thinking about English Canada and its identity? What degree of recognition do we need to give to the diversity of ethnic groups making up this country? What are the limits beyond which such recognition threatens to splinter us? What finally of the multicultural presence in relationship to that of two other important groups, aboriginal peoples and English Canada's francophone minorities?

Let us be honest. Multiculturalism is a very new theme in some ways and a radical departure from the way in which Canada outside Quebec was viewed by a majority of English-speaking Canadians at least down to World War II. The Loyalist motif was an important one in the formulation of an English-Canadian sense of itself — British, monarchical, predominantly Protestant. The British colonists of Nova Scotia, New Brunswick, Lower Canada, and Upper Canada were not all descendants of those who had fled the Thirteen Colonies at the time of the American Revolution; but the Loyalists played a role in 19th- and early-20th-century English-Canadian history not unlike the mythic one of Mayflower and Pilgrim Fathers for the United States.

The symbols of Canada — flag, anthem ("God Save the King/Queen" alongside "O Canada"), governor general — harked on this British/Loyalist past. Generations of schoolchildren, whether of British background or not, were socialized to respect the signal contribution Loyalists had made and the essentially British affinities and character of Canada. That this socialization helped to differentiate Canada from the United States is unquestionable; that it reflected what was for long a demographic reality — the preponderance of those of British stock in the population of Canada outside Quebec — is also true. That it could, however, provide a unifying theme for all time, particularly as Canada's ties to Britain weakened and the non-British component of English Canada's population increased, was much less obvious.

Nations, much like individuals, evolve and change. A person in his/her youth is not the same as that person in middle age. The credo of one's grandparents or parents is not necessarily one's own. To try to freeze a certain conception of English Canada, for instance, a Loyalist one, through time was therefore an impossibility. Recognizing this reality is not a matter of disparaging the past or denying its significance. It is simply one of getting on with mapping the realities of late-20th-century Canada and of recognizing just how much Canadian society has changed.

And changed it has. One cannot have an ever-growing admixture of population from the most wide-ranging of sources without this affecting our sense of who we are. One could hardly expect generation after generation of immigrant to line up meekly to one side while those who had come here first maintained a privileged claim to define the identity of us all. As citizenship rights were extended to people of ever different backgrounds, the face of Canada outside Quebec ceased to be British.

It does not follow that the *English Canada* of today bears no relationship whatsoever to that of the past; nor, more saliently, that it is little more than the sum of its multiple ethnic or cultural parts.

No nationality can be forged *ex novo* without some feeling by its members for what had come before, however each generation chooses to reinterpret this. No new nationality represents a purely physical combination of elements, each discrete and unaltered in the process. Rather, the process of national development is analagous to a chemical reaction, in which people of different backgrounds interact with one another, losing something of their previous identities as they forge a new, collective sense of self.

That collective sense of self in late-20th-century English Canada can and must reflect the varied backgrounds of our population. In that sense, we are a profoundly multicultural society, one that will continue to evolve as current and future waves of immigration come to be absorbed into the social fabric. No single ethnic, cultural, or religious group has exclusive right to call itself Canadian or English Canadian; no group, as was done in the past to Japanese Canadians, can be read out by the majority as un-Canadian.

What does recognition of our diversity entail? The right, at a minimum, for our different cultural communities to cultivate those features of their background that they wish to preserve and foster. This right encompasses a large range of things from religious practice to the use of language of origin within their community institutions. Recognition is also secured as members of different ethnic communities are elected, appointed, and hired to mainstream positions at the municipal, provincial, and federal level. There can be no better testament to having "made it" within the larger English-Canadian society.

There is also a case for public support for certain multicultural activities. The teaching of heritage languages — in addition to the normal curriculum — in schools with large numbers of children from particular ethnic communities is one example. Some funding for community centres, ethnic language newspapers, and the like is another. And the provision by public agencies of relevant information in different languages spoken within the community is yet a third.

So far so good. But there comes a point beyond which multiculturalism could become a threat to the viability of an English-Canadian nationality. If we think of other nationalities around the world, language is a central facet of their makeup. What distinguishes Ukrainians from Russians, Poles from Czechs, Norwegians from Swedes, Koreans from Chinese is, to no small degree, language. While multinational federations, with some difficulty as the Canadian or Belgian or Indian cases suggest, can recognize two or more official languages, there are no nationalities that do not have a language that they speak. The alternative is to risk creating a Tower of Babel.

It is very important, as was argued earlier, to distinguish between language and ethnicity when using a term such as *English Canada*. What I have in mind when using the term *English Canada* throughout this book is a territorial community, essentially outside Quebec, with English as its dominant language. Neither more nor less. This formulation does not imply that the only form of culture in English-speaking Canada must be English-derived or based, or that our plethora of ethnic communities be denied their identities. But it does mean very clearly that immigrants and ethnic communities living in English Canada understand that their languages can never aspire to the status of an official language. And it further means that they accept to be part of an evolving society in which a culture based on English has been the prevailing one.

There are a number of other restrictions that must be placed on too broadly based a multicultural definition of English Canada. Ours is an ongoing society with certain political traditions developed in the 19th century and furthered in the 20th. Reference has already been made to conservative, liberal, and social democratic strains in English-Canadian political culture. In the same vein, we can speak of traditions of constitutionalism, parliamentarism, rule of law, individual rights, and the like. These are not principles with which most English-speaking Canadians would be prepared to dispense, at least not without some very persuasive arguments. They, therefore, represent touchstones of Canadian identity that immigrants buy into by coming to this country. English Canada is not some tabula rasa or blank sheet to be recast every time new cultural communities come along. These different communities must themselves make serious efforts to accommodate themselves to the ethos of the larger society. In asking this of our different ethnic communities, English-speaking Canadians would be asking no more than any other nationality in the world.

Two particular groups do not fit the multicultural rubric in the way over a hundred others do. The first, our aboriginal peoples, were here before the coming of the Europeans; as was suggested in the previous chapter, they were dispossessed of lands and identities and were merely involuntary participants in much of the history that was to follow. Accordingly they have claims to recognition as nations, with languages and cultures of their own, and to a distinct political status that other ethnic communities, whatever their origins or numbers, do not.

The second group is the francophone minority within English Canada, especially larger groupings such as the Acadians in New Brunswick, Franco-Ontarians, and the like. Within Canada as it is currently constituted, both English and French enjoy the status of official languages. Moreover, Canada as a federal state has involved a de facto pact between the English-speaking majority concentrated outside Quebec and a French-speaking majority in Quebec. We do not have to sanction this "agreement" with the term *compact theory;* the fact remains that English–French harmony has been essential to the functioning of the Canadian ensemble.

What happens, however, if we move in an asymmetrical or confederal direction to reflect better the national sentiments of Québécois, aboriginal peoples, and English Canadians? Quite clearly, official bilingualism would have little place in a Canada where Quebec and English Canada were largely autonomous from each other. One would still preserve it in those areas of jurisdiction, say foreign affairs, defence, trade, that they agreed to share; or within such provinces as New Brunswick that chose to define themselves as bilingual. But within Quebec or English Canada as a whole, the dominant language and, therefore, the official one, would be French or English.

Do the minorities, anglophones in Quebec, francophones outside, go by the boards? One would trust not — on historical grounds, on moral, and on political ones, as well. For over two centuries, French- or English-language minorities have existed in the two majority-language communities. For a long time, the English in Quebec were, indisputably, in a stronger position than the French outside Quebec; but over the past 30 years, the relative position of the francophone communities in the rest of Canada has improved, where education and services in their own language are concerned. It would be a tragedy of the first order if there were to be a significant whittling away of minority rights in the future, with English Canada and Quebec descending to the level of ethnic intolerance and conflict we have been seeing in the Balkans or Central Asia.

A fortiori, if it is our intention to have an ongoing Canada–Quebec arrangement of some kind, minority language rights become quite pivotal. It will be impossible to work out alternative models for Canada if there is even a hint of intolerance toward language minorities. Our recent experience with both Bill 178 and English-Canadian backlash teaches us that much. We may not keep the rubric of the Official Languages Act, but we will certainly need to have constitutional protections, both in English Canada and in Quebec, for these minorities. Just as Quebec can be said to include an anglophone community as a constituent part of its identity, so francophone communities are a constituent part of English Canada's. And they should not, therefore, be put on the same footing as other ethnic communities.

Let me, then, offer some parting thoughts on the question of multiculturalism. In one way, multiculturalism opens up wonderful opportunities to tap the diversity of Canada's ethnic heritage, itself a microcosm, more and more, of the planet as a whole. To the degree that English Canada, moreover, has become less European or less white, to the degree that it has shed a predominantly British Isles tropism, it has gone beyond ethnicity in laying the foundations for national identity.

Such developments, in my opinion, are reason for celebration. English-Canadian society represents a remarkable amalgam of cultural communities and people; wisely it does not require that each of these surrender its identity in order to become Canadian. If English Canada is to develop a sense of itself as a nation, it will be through continuing to foster such open-mindedness in the years to come.

Where I would draw the line, however, is with a multiculturalism that might seek to deny a specifically Canadian or English-Canadian identity altogether. In a world where nationality remains a primary source of identity — whatever the 21st or 25th centuries may bring — English Canadians must be careful not to deny themselves the ability to think of themselves as a nation. National identity requires a primacy for English against any other language; a minimal sense of our past and of the political traditions we have developed; a sense of place here in the northern part of North America and nowhere else. English Canada is multicultural, but it must be based on something more than multiculturalism.

8

Region and Nation

Between the continent and the historic village
is an area sometimes larger, sometimes smaller,
than the political state. It is the human region.
— LEWIS MUMFORD

EVEN IF QUEBEC AND ABORIGINAL LANDS were not politically part of Canada, we would still have to confront the question of region and regionalism within English Canada. In a continent-wide ensemble that began on the Atlantic Seaboard and St. Lawrence basin and gradually spread to encompass the Great Lakes, northern Ontario, the Prairies, the Rocky Divide, the Pacific Coast, and the territories, a uniform sense of nation would not come easily. Local communities rooted in geographical spaces for the most part unconnected with similar spaces 200, let alone 1,500 miles, away were very much the rule; particular patterns of settlement characterized the Maritimes, Ontario, and points west; different resource or staple industries underlay the political economies of each region.

At what moment, one might ask, would a sense of country larger than region begin to emerge? What were and are some of the regional barriers to the development of national consciousness within English Canada? How do forces such as regionalism, nationalism, or internationalism interact? And what are the prospects, in thinking English

Canada, of balancing off centripetal with centrifugal forces, centralizing with decentralizing ones?

The formal birth of Canada is easy enough to date. More complex
is the question of whether one can really speak of a Canadian (let
alone English Canadian) nation as far back as 1867 when the
Dominion of Canada was created. There was something missing at
the mythic level where the British North American colonies were
concerned, for instance, a radical break with Great Britain as had
occurred to the south of us in 1776, as well as a clear vision of a new
nationality and what it hoped to accomplish in the northern part of
North America.

The only area of even moderate population concentration stradled
the language boundary between Quebec and Ontario. Otherwise the
business of state-building was caught up with an interminable search
for railway links, first between the Maritimes and the Canadas, then
between central Canada and the west. The need to bind together
regions, however thinly and fitfully, would dominate Canadian
politics down to the outbreak of World War I. For there was nothing
predestined about British Columbia's inclusion in Canada or about
the filling in of the old Hudson Bay lands with homesteaders from
Europe in an emerging wheat economy.

The creation of a federal state structure, the railway and tariff
policies that accompanied it, the vigorous pursuit of immigration
from Europe in the boom years of the early 1900s, helped impart a
more national dimension to Canadian life. So, too, more tellingly,
would Canadian participation in World War I, a coming-of-age
where questions of sovereignty and national consciousness were
concerned. A somewhat peripheral community found itself
caught up in the conflict that tore the Old World apart, destroying
its dynastic empires forever. Nationalism of the most atavistic sort
had been unleashed, and a struggle for domination, and for
recognition, as well, was being waged on the killing grounds of
Europe. It is no accident that Vimy Ridge is sometimes seen as
Canada's baptism by fire as an actor in its own right, something
formalized at the Peace Conference at Versailles and in the newly
created League of Nations.

Yet there were ambiguities and contradictions surrounding such developments. First and foremost, it was by no means evident, as World War I was to confirm, that Quebec national sentiment paralleled that of English-speaking Canada. Indeed, the imposition of conscription in 1917, far more than the earlier cleavages over the hanging of Louis Riel or the Manitoba School Question, threatened to tear Canada apart, so that it might be more appropriate to speak of the emergence of an English-Canadian national consciousness during World War I rather than of a Canadian consciousness *tout court*. Something of the same difference, moreover, would surface during World War II, as the conscription crisis of 1942 would reveal.

Second, and more pertinent to the theme of this chapter, once peace had returned in late 1918 and internal preoccupations were again the order of the day, regional fissures resurfaced. The 1920s saw the Maritime Rights Movement, expressing profound disillusionment with the "poor sister" role of the Atlantic provinces within Canadian Confederation. The 1920s and 1930s saw a series of third parties on the Prairies — the Progressives, the United Farmers of Alberta, the CCF, Social Credit; each in its own ways embodied regional unhappiness with a "peripheral" position within Canada and with economic domination by railways, grain companies, and banks with links to central Canada. Regional discontent and the class-based grievances of grain farmers fused dramatically, sparking the most telling examples of populist politics in 20th-century English Canada. In British Columbia, a fair amount of the language of provincial politics from Duff Pattullo to W. A. C. Bennett and beyond would be that of a region distant from and ignored by the federal government, and of a region far less dependent on protectionism and the domestic Canadian market than Ontario or Quebec.

Provincial politicans were quick to use the spheres of jurisdiction awarded them under the British North America Act to resist encroachments by the federal government. Such resistance might flag in periods of economic hardship like the Great Depression or under the exceptional conditions of war. But it stood in the way of too centralizing a shift of the pendulum, whatever the desire of federal politicians and civil servants, the needs of the economy, or the mood of English-Canadian opinion itself. The fact that the same provincial premiers or parties might hold power through long decades further reinforced their ability to present themselves as the defenders and spokespersons for their regions.

There was, therefore, within the very logic of Canadian federalism a significant barrier to the development of a uniform national consciousness. The reality of centre-periphery relations through the first century of Confederation would make the Atlantic and western provinces profoundly suspicious of many of the actions of the federal government; the concentration of population, finance, and manufacturing in Ontario and Quebec was a further source of friction. That the resource base of Atlantic Canada, the Prairies, or British Columbia differed significantly from that of central Canada; that education from the primary through to the postsecondary level was firmly under provincial jurisdiction; that a good deal of public works and, for that matter, social assistance was under provincial control further contributed to a regional or provincial sense of community rather than a national one.

The variegated economic base of the regions might also lead to quite different patterns of integration with the outside world. The markets for British Columbia lumber, Alberta gas and oil, Saskatchewan potash, or Maritime sea products (when the fish were still there!) lay only partially within Canada itself; in most cases, the American market loomed larger, instilling a continental pattern onto the Canadian economy long before the Canada–U.S. Free Trade Agreement of 1988 had been framed. In more recent years, the markets for Canadian resources might increasingly lie with the rising economies of East Asia, even as Europe had once constituted the primary Canadian export market for wheat. Regional economic interests could impart their own directions to provincial politics; interregional conflicts and conflicts between the provinces and the federal government, for instance, over the pricing of oil and gas during the energy crisis of the 1970s and the National Energy Program, might be the upshot.

If regional and provincial loyalties were potentially so important, however, what was the source of national feelings? What has made a majority of English-speaking Canadians see themselves as Canadians and not merely British Columbians, Ontarians, or Nova Scotians? For national sentiment clearly does exist in English Canada, despite

the federal-provincial division of powers, powerful provincial bro-
kers, or differing regional economic bases.

In truth, the proponents of regionalism within English Canada,
in direct contrast to the supporters of Quebec nationalism in the
contemporary period, have seldom thought of their regions in
nation-state terms. (Admittedly there may have been a few voices for
separation in Alberta at the height of the National Energy Policy
debate, but only a few.) Invariably the call has been for a better deal
for a particular province or region within the Canadian political
framework, better political representation in central institutions like
Cabinet or Parliament, greater sensitivity to regional economic interests, and equal treatment of all provinces where ownership of
resources was concerned. A sense of region does not in and of itself
translate into a sense of nation, not when there are unifying historical, cultural, and linguistic bonds.

These bonds, one could argue, do indeed exist for English Canada.
What began with Vimy or the League of Nations did not expire with
the Depression or World War II. Economic hardship in the Dirty
Thirties did not spare any region; nor did the solutions lie at the local
level as opposed to a vigorous set of policies at the federal one,
namely, the creation of the Canadian Wheat Board, the Bank of
Canada, a Canada-wide unemployment insurance system. As far as
the Maritimes, Ontario, or the West were concerned, there were no
noticeable differences in attitudes toward the war effort in the years
1939–45; if anything, this period, much like 1914–18, represented
the further cementing of a common English-Canadian consciousness
through a common pride in the military and economic contributions
Canada was making to the Allied cause. Dieppe and Normandy,
Hong Kong and Italy became part of Canadian war lore, along with
air strikes on Germany, transatlantic naval convoys, pilot training
for the Commonwealth, and much besides. There was no possible
questioning of Canada's rightful place as a founding member of the
United Nations.

To sketch post-World War II features of English-Canadian national consciousness in a few short strokes would be difficult. One
could do worse than begin with the cultural. Already in the 1930s,
the creation of the CBC had heralded a concern for a coast-to-coast

broadcasting system unbeholden to the American networks. The National Film Board, created during the war, gave further voice to specifically Canadian concerns in the relatively new medium of film. Few matters seemed to galvanize Canadian public opinion more in the postwar period, one of overwhelming American influence across the board, than that of culture. The Royal Commission on the Arts, Letters, and Sciences of 1949–51, the Canada Council created in 1957, policies to protect the Canadian publishing industry or to foster Canadianization in the universities in the 1970s were some of its manifestations. The regional pole was certainly a factor in cultural matters — regionally based broadcasters and publishers, dance or theatre companies, provincially administered systems of postsecondary education. Yet few could deny the simultaneous existence of nationally read authors, a theatre repertoire, or film industry that crossed regional lines, core Canadian elements to the humanities, social sciences, and many of the professional disciplines regardless of university or province.

Politically one can underline other commonalities in the English-Canadian experience. External ties such as the United Nations, NATO, or the Commonwealth helped to mute strictly regional loyalties; Canadian policies with respect to international peacekeeping, apartheid, and a whole range of east-west and north-south issues were clearly national in character. Internally events such as the Pipeline Debate of 1956, the 1965 ruckus over the flag, the October Crisis, or the constitutional patriation battle of 1980–81 focused public attention on the federal level. The move to the welfare state, which had begun with wartime measures such as unemployment insurance and family allowances, was carried significantly further with the Canada Pension Plan, medicare, and the Canada Assistance Plan of the 1960s. These assured common standards across the country regardless of region, a key factor in the formulation of a common English-Canadian identity. (One might note the establishment of an administratively separate Quebec Pension Plan in 1964, heralding the deeper symbolic division between Quebec and English Canada.) The Charter of Rights and Freedoms of 1982 helped give many English Canadians a common notion of citizenship transcending region, while the constitutional bickering unleashed by Meech

Lake and Charlottetown forced English Canadians, wherever they lived, to begin to define themselves and their aspirations in contra-distinction to Quebec's. This account does not aim to downplay real divisions in English-Canadian opinion — over the Free Trade Agreement, to cite a recent example, over the earlier shedding of the British symbolism in anthem or flag, over the nature and extent of our military alliances during the Cold War period. But the fault lines on questions of this sort rarely ran along regional lines.

Economically, despite the obvious southward tug and pull on English Canada's different regions, there is an east-west pattern of integration at work. Major financial, industrial, transportation, and communications enterprises have operations and directorships that span regional lines. Trade unions provide similar linkages where labour is concerned. Fiscal and monetary policy, trade policy, agricultural support programs, labour market training, unemployment insurance, regional equalization programs are determined at a Canada-wide level. So while resources may be under provincial control, helping to create regionally based economies, there are important countervailing forces promoting a more national economic outlook. Continental and global integration, moreover, have given bilateral and multilateral mechanisms and institutions — for example, the dispute resolution mechanisms negotiated under the Canada–U.S. Free Trade Agreement, or the General Agreement on Tariffs and Trade (GATT), the International Monetary Fund (IMF), the World Bank, and the Organization for Economic Cooperation and Development (OECD) — greater salience, further reinforcing the national, as opposed to purely regional, pole.

Finally, something must be said about English Canada's social fabric. The movement of population within English-speaking Canada, from the Atlantic provinces to Ontario, for example, from Ontario and the Prairies to British Columbia, from British Columbia to other provinces, helps reinforce a sense of common nationality, undercutting purely regional identities. The large number of immigrants of diverse origins populating Canada's major centres, the common linkages that members of the same ethnic group have with others of similar backgrounds across Canada, serves to weaken purely regional tropisms in yet another way. Canada-wide social movements, religious and cultural organizations, political parties, occupational and interest groups, for their part, help to solidify national, as opposed to purely regional loyalties, within English Canada.

So to see Canada, and English Canada in particular, as little more than a "community of communities," as Joe Clark or the Pepin-Robarts Commission of the late 1970s were wont to do, is to seriously miss the mark. To see English Canada as nothing but a collection of regions, each with a fixed and fervent sense of itself and but tangential commitment to Canada as a whole, is to err even more. Quebec may well act in such a fashion — one of the reasons we need to rethink profoundly our relations with that society. The sense of nation within English Canada is too deeply rooted and goes back too far in time for any of its regions to share such aspirations.

It does not follow that regional sentiments do not matter. Their significance for a continent-wide state like Canada was acknowledged earlier. Nor is it the case that the view of nation may not vary significantly from one region to another. The Atlantic provinces, as English Canada's oldest settled region, bring a conservatism and emphasis on continuity to their vision of Canada. Ontario, as English Canada's most populous province and financial and manufacturing centre (despite the recent ravages of deindustrialization), has played a linchpin role in fostering an east-west, as opposed to purely continental, set of relationships. The Prairies have contributed a strong dose of populism to English-Canadian political culture, spawned third parties both of the right and left, and helped pioneer a more multicultural and less British sense of nation. British Columbia, for its part, was long the periphery of the periphery, a Canadian California to which those fleeing the old metropolises might venture. Fortune-seekers and visionaries, robber barons and militant unionists, loggers and environmentalists lived or still live cheek by jowl. And with Canada's increasing ties across the Pacific — the Mediterranean of the 21st century — and a burgeoning Asiatic population of its own, British Columbia helps impart an Asian Pacific dimension to English Canada as a whole.

Region and nation within English Canada, it shoud be stressed, must be kept in balance. There is little to be gained by lurching off in a strongly centralizing direction, denying the legitimacy of regional identities and, in the process, arrogating provincial powers into federal hands. But decentralizing measures, of the sort that Meech Lake and Charlottetown incarnated, threatened to enhance the forces of regionalism and provincial loyalty at the expense of a shared English-Canadian identity. This sense of identity helps explain the significant opposition both constitutional agreements evoked in English Canada and the resonance of Trudeau's defence of federal powers, even for those who questioned his position on Quebec.

We may well want, even need, to rethink the federal-provincial division of powers in the future, where the internal English-Canadian relationship is concerned. Certain areas of jurisdiction, for example, child care, may well belong in provincial hands along with elementary and secondary education; conversely postsecondary education would surely gain from an enhanced federal role. Environmental jurisdiction needs to be redefined in light of the increasingly global dimension of such problems, on the one hand, and of the need for local and regional solutions on the other. There is no hard and fast rule as to whether federal or provincial powers, in a particular area, serve the population of English Canada best, and we shall have to see some of the same flexibility in charting the future allocation of powers between the two levels of government as we have seen in the past.

What is crucial, however, in thinking English Canada (as opposed to Canada as a whole) is to free ourselves from the bane that Quebec, ever since the Quiet Revolution, has introduced into our political life, namely, the incessant demand for increased provincial power. If Quebec is a nation, as I have argued above, there is a strong case for giving it greatly enhanced powers within a looser Canadian arrangement. But there is no such case for giving enhanced powers to the provinces of English Canada or for watering down those national features that we, as English Canadians, share. Quite the opposite course is called for, especially if we are to set out on new and untested arrangements both with Quebec and with our aboriginal peoples in the not too distant future.

An English Canada that is not at peace with its regions, in which each of these regions does not find space for its own identity, will not long endure. But an English Canada where regions begin to think of themselves, much as Quebec does, as embryonic nations, will have even less of a future. Despite the globalization we are witnessing in the economic arena, and real limits to the sovereignty of states, national identities remain of critical importance in the OECD countries, in the ex-Communist ones, and in the Third World. We will either be a nation, with a commitment to something larger than region and a sense of identity as English Canadians, or we will have lost our very reason to exist.

9

The Democratic Deficit: Breaking the Mould

LTHOUGH WE HAVE HAD representative institutions since the 18th century and responsible forms of government since the middle of the 19th century, I would argue that Canadians, by and large, have not known popular sovereignty in its fullest measure. The process by which the British North America Act came to be framed involved closed-door meetings of the elected politicians of the day; the constitutional proposals in question were never submitted directly to the people of the then colonies for approval, but were passed as a statute of the British Parliament; and within the framework of government established at Confederation nary a mention was made of the Canadian people or of democracy as such.

True, Canadians exercised de facto control over legislative, and to a lesser degree, executive power. As heirs to the British system of government, they acquired a broad degree of male suffrage (extended to women in 1921) in parliamentary elections. Political parties and their leaders had little choice but to curry popular favour both to win power and to maintain it. And there was the possibility, when the old-line Conservative or Liberal parties failed in their tasks, for new parties, at both the provincial and federal levels, to come along, as was increasingly the case from the 1920s on.

Yet the notion of power resting directly with the people was seen as something alien, even incompatible, with a British-derived notion of sovereignty. Such ideas may have been put forward by the

Levellers during the English Civil War years of the 1640s. They may have found their place in constitutions of the American or French variety, derived from the revolutions of the late 18th century. In Britain, from 1689 on, and in dominions like Canada, sovereignty was seen to be vested in king/queen-in-Parliament and nowhere else.

This history helps to explain some of the awkwardness English Canadians have had to face in comparing their situation with that of their neighbours. The Jacksonian persuasion of the 1830s had put the *demos* front and centre in American politics. The populist movement of the late 19th century introduced referenda, the initiative, and recall into many state constitutions. The 20th century saw public opinion and, at times, the media playing a robust role in the making and unmaking of presidents and administrations.

My account does not aim to overlook glaring weaknesses in the operation of American democracy, for instance, the wholesale influence of money in political affairs, the lingering effects of racism, a chauvinism and intolerance accompanying the American rise to world power. There could be no mistaking, however, the democratic heritage that underlay the American experience, one broadened and deepened by the travails of the Civil War or by the opening of the United States to settlement by successive waves of immigrants.

There were echoes of American populism in western Canada during the early 20th century in the form of agrarian-based parties and movements. Immigration also helped transform the face of English Canada, somewhat loosening the older hierarchies. By and large, nonetheless, English Canadians have experienced less by way of popular forms of politics than Americans. Political leaders, both federal and provincial, have had long runs in office — one of the vices of a parliamentary system. Our parties have had more of a stranglehold over the political agenda. And, for a long time, dissent had only a limited toehold in English-Canadian society. It is hard to say how much of this pattern should be attributed to the evolutionary, top-down manner in which Canada came to be created; how much to the peace, order, and good government tradition with which we were saddled; and how much to monarchical as opposed to republican forms of government. But there has been something of a democratic deficit to Canadian public life for much of our history.

From time to time, popular movements — farmers, workers, women, aboriginal, environmental — have made their mark felt. And occasionally the Canadian people have been consulted directly on matters political. There have been three referenda or plebiscites at the Canada-wide level — one on prohibition in 1898, one on conscription in 1942, and one on the Charlottetown Accord in 1992. The infrequency with which these have been held and the lack of consensus between English Canada and Quebec in the first two (and, despite surface commonality, in the third) attest to their marginal place in the larger scheme of things. That they embody a counter-legitimacy to that of our elected politicians at both levels of government does, nonetheless, bear underlining.

In a world of nation-states with their far-flung populations and large territories, direct democracy of the type practised in Athens in the fifth and fourth centuries B.C. becomes an impossibility. At best, it can be practised in small-scale communities of the rural Swiss canton or New England town meeting variety. Or it can be approximated in the practice of referenda.

Not all issues lend themselves equally well to resolution by referendum. Major changes in a state's constitutional arrangements may be of such an order; so, too, many changes in its external relations, for instance, membership by different European countries in the European Community (and some might argue Canadian participation in NAFTA). What referenda allow in such cases is an expression of popular sentiment that is not frozen along traditional party lines and that is a clear verdict on the matter at hand.

In the case of Quebec, the 1980 referendum on sovereignty-association played a clarifying role. Although there were significant differences of opinion between the proponents and opponents of sovereignty regarding the exact wording of the referendum question, on one thing there was broad consensus. A decision of such significance should not be made by a government elected in the course of an ordinary election but ought to be put directly to the population as a whole. The change in the status of Quebec that sovereignty (or sovereignty-association) would entail was so far-ranging as to need the legitimacy of popular approval.

Such support was not forthcoming in May 1980. But the precedent of the referendum did serve an important function, helping to legitimize the notion of direct popular approval for any major constitutional changes, in English Canada no less than in Quebec. In a significant way, Meech Lake suffered from the absence of such a transparent process of ratification. In the run-up to Charlottetown, the notion of referendum (often accompanied by constituent assembly) as the sole legitimate means of sanctioning constitutional change gained overwhelming support.

The democratic deficit runs deeply in English-Canadian society at the moment. It runs deeply across the Western world as a whole, as the recent European experience with the Maastricht Treaty would also suggest. There is growing hostility to decisions made by political elites that do not reflect the aspirations of the population at large. There is a suspicion of traditional ways of doing politics that has led to populist upsurges in countries as diverse as Italy, France, Denmark, the United States, and Canada. The success of the Reform Party in capturing votes from across the political spectrum reflects this discontent.

What our recent constitutional experience teaches us is the impossibility of arriving at workable alternatives without a large measure of grass-roots participation in the political process. There were hints of this concern in some of the Spicer Commission hearings and in several of the constitutional conferences, for example, Halifax, Calgary, and Toronto, where so-called ordinary Canadians mingled with experts and a diversity of interest group representatives. Somewhere on the road to Charlottetown the imperatives of elite accommodation won out over everything else. Still, the lesson we ought to retain from such forums is the need for the broadest possible consultation in discussing the future of English Canada and with it the future of Canada.

Just as Quebec's use of the referendum may have served English Canada as an example, there may be a further element in the recent Quebec experience worth our attention. Back in 1966–67, when the first wave of Quebec nationalism was cresting, Jacques-Yvan Morin, a constitutional law professor at the University of Montreal (and future Parti Québécois Cabinet minister), had the idea of convening an Estates General of French Canada. The term *Estates General* referred back to the parliamentary body that had existed in ancien régime France and whose convocation in 1789, after a 175-year hiatus, helped trigger the French Revolution. It is striking, however, that the term *French Canada,* rather than *Quebec,* was used as the name of the proposed body.

The Estates General of French Canada was not convened by any government; nor was it an official decision-making organization. It did, however, bring together some 2,000 delegates from a diversity of social, cultural, economic, and political organizations, primarily in Quebec, but also representing francophones outside Quebec. They met in Montreal, following a series of regional conferences, to debate a number of questions involving the future of French-speaking Canada. The nationalist position tended to prevail, that is, one favouring the view of Quebec as a French-speaking nation within Canada. But a range of options, from traditionalist and religious to secular and avant-garde, was reflected within the body; and its deliberations helped advance the general level of political conscious-ness in Quebec.

We could do worse than emulate this experience if we want to help launch a far-ranging debate within English Canada about its own identity. Why not an Estates General of English Canada with delegates from the nine predominantly English-speaking provinces, the two territories and, for good measure, the anglophone minority of Quebec? If the model of the constitutional forums were to be followed, we might want to have major social, economic, and cultural organizations represented. To these might be added a small number of representatives from the different political parties. The lion's share of representation, however, would go to ordinary English Canadians, reflecting the gender, age, occupational, and ethnic diversity of English Canada.

Governments should not take the initiative in convening such a gathering. Ideally that role should be played by a representative cross-sample of academics, artists, businesspeople, trade unionists, ethnic communities, and women's organizations, aiming at as broadly based and open-ended a debate as possible. Forums could be organized at the local and provincial levels first; ultimately a larger gathering (or gatherings) at the level of English Canada as a whole would follow.

Would an Estates General for English Canada be setting the stage for a wholesale restructuring of the Canadian federation? Who knows? One thing it would allow, however, is a frank exchange of views among English-speaking Canadians in the absence of Quebec, something we have not really experienced in our history. It would allow for the exploration of a whole series of issues, including the nature of our relations with Quebec, the bonds that tie (or do not tie) English Canada together, views on the federal-provincial division of powers, on relations with the United States, on multiculturalism, bilingualism, aboriginal identities, and so on. Such a forum would make possible a wide-ranging debate on English-Canadian identity — a veritable first.

Like our recent constitutional debate, it might serve as a useful step toward greater democratization. If there is to be any new thinking about English Canada (or about Canada as a whole), such ideas cannot simply be dropped from above on a passive populace. They must themselves reflect the real life experiences and concerns of the 20 million or so inhabitants of Canada who define themselves as neither Québécois nor aboriginals.

Much as there is a democratic deficit in the functioning of liberal democratic regimes such as our own, there is a national deficit of sorts when it comes to English-Canadian reflections on Canada. Until now the greatest impetus for change has come from Quebec, with demands ranging from significantly greater autonomy to outright independence. More recently, some of the calls for change have come from aboriginal organizations such as the Assembly of First Nations with its support for aboriginal self-government. What then of English Canada? Should it be committed to holding on to the status quo at any price? Is it prepared to pose the question of its own identity within a federation where two other groups (or at least majorities within each) see themselves in national terms? Is it open to possible changes to our federation down the line, provided its own interests and identity can be advanced?

Such questions need to be addressed in the years ahead. My own inclination, as the reader will have guessed, leads me to reject the status quo and to favour a Yes answer to the last two questions. Not everyone will agree. But we do need a debate on the English-Canadian side and, for once, I propose that we not wait for Quebec to force the issue after its next election or when it gets caught up in a possible referendum in 1995. Perhaps, just perhaps, we can decide that it is in our own interest as English Canadians to embark on such a discussion in advance of future developments. The Bloc Québécois presence in Ottawa should surely spur us on. If so, in this more democratic age, what better way to go about a debate than through some such forum as an Estates General (or Consultative Assembly, to coin a more English-sounding term) for English Canada, even if for symbolic reasons we decide to convene it in Charlottetown?

10

English Canada, Quebec, and Aboriginal Peoples: Alternative Scenarios

C ANADA IS AT A CROSSROADS. The vision of a single unhyphenated nationality binding all the inhabitants of this country from coast-to-coast lives on among a majority of English-speaking Canadians (and a minority of Québécois and aboriginal people, as well). It surfaces in the vocabulary of Canadian politics with constant references to the Canadian nation, national parties, national programs, the national capital, and so on. It moves a large number of Canadians, both old and new, to identify with the rights and freedoms of the charter, with the Trudeau-derived vision of a bilingual and multicultural Canadian federation, and with a Canada in which all provinces are equal. It explains the antipathy toward special status for Quebec or for aboriginal peoples that underlay a good deal of the No vote in English Canada in the referendum of October 1992. And it suggests that many will resist the underlying premise of this book, namely, the need to start thinking about English Canada as a sociological nation in its own right.

There is a calculated risk behind what I would call the stand-pat position. It rests on the premise that demands from Quebec for a fundamental restructuring of the Canadian federation along the lines of two (or more) nations are bluffs; that Canada survived the election of a Parti Québécois government in 1976 and its referendum gambit of 1980; that we have similarly survived the Meech Lake imbroglio, the Allaire Report, and the mixed blessings of Charlottetown; and that we shall similarly survive Lucien Bouchard and the Bloc Québécois. Quebec nationalism has been known to wane as well as to wax. All English Canadians need to do is show a bit of backbone, a clear refusal to play the autonomist/sovereigntist game. A majority of Québécois, aware that they have far more to lose than to gain from the breakup of Canada, will get back to more immediate preoccupations like economic restructuring or milking the federal system for all it is worth. Canada will continue much as before for another 125 years, with the occasional crisis to test our resolve.

Let me acknowledge that this is indeed one possible scenario; that the crisis of the past three decades where Quebec is concerned may have simply been one of transition to modernity or postmodernity; that in the more global and North America-wide capitalism that now guides our collective destiny, sovereignty is yesterday's idea and nationalism a fading dream. Certainly a good number of English Canadians, especially in the corporate and business sector, would view Canadian nationalism this way; and some of their confrères in Quebec share such an analysis of Quebec nationalism.

The danger, of course, is that they are wrong, that the revival of nationalism that we are witnessing in more benighted regions of the earth — parts of Western and Central Europe, the Balkans, the Caucasus, Central Asia, the Indian subcontinent, the Arab world — is of more than passing relevance to us. Moreover, along the lines of my earlier argument, if multinational federations such as the Soviet Union, Yugoslavia, and Czechoslovakia have fallen apart, and others like Belgium and India lurch from crisis to crisis, can we confidently assume our invulnerability? Especially in light of the election outcome of October 1993?

Back in the 1920s, a Canadian senator, Raoul Dandurand, speaking at the League of Nations, suggested that Canada lived in a fireproof house. There was nothing fireproof for Canadians (or Americans) about the rise of Hitler, or for that matter of a Japan bent on conquering East Asia. Nor would we be wise to play ostrich today with the nationalist pressures that threaten to splinter Canada.

If we wish to avoid unanticipated crises and sudden-death

meltdowns, it might, after all, make sense to sketch alternative scenarios. The status quo may be comfortable enough for many in English Canada, but if it fails to satisfy a majority in Quebec or allay aboriginal discontent, it will simply not endure. So what are other possible scenarios?

One variant, which underlay both Meech and Charlottetown, is that of wholesale devolution of power to the provinces. In attempting to address Quebec demands for greater autonomy, one will place limits on federal spending powers; transfer jurisdiction over labour market training, housing, tourism, and culture to provinces that wish this; and give the provinces leverage over federal institutions like the Supreme Court or the Bank of Canada. Whatever new jurisdictions might be offered to Quebec would be offered to the other provinces. The price of renewing the Canadian federation would thus be a significant weakening of the federal government. Aboriginal self-government might be added to such an arrangement, although provinces might prove more zealous guardians of their jurisdictions and territory vis-à-vis aboriginals than the federal government itself.

The problem with this variant is twofold. On the one hand, it weakens the cohesion of the Canadian pole, opening the door to a balkanization of identities. The provincial and regional poles would loom ever larger, economically, culturally, politically, even within English-speaking Canada, and the notion of common citizenship and shared national standards would quickly fray. There are English Canadians, especially on the political right, who would buy into such a vision of country. But there is no small number of English Canadians, especially on the political centre and left, who would not. The formula of devolution is, therefore, extremely divisive where English Canada itself is concerned.

Second, the unintended consequence of giving to all provinces powers that Quebec in particular seeks is to make Quebec itself less satisfied in the end. Instead of symbolic recognition of its distinctiveness, Quebec ends up, much as it began, as one province among ten. True, it may choose to exercise certain powers that others do not, but its status falls short of the sociological nationhood that political leaders ever since Jean Lesage have been seeking. So devolution does not solve the deeper problems of recognition that gnaw

at our federation. (Aboriginal self-government, if too narrowly cir-
cumscribed, might also fail to meet the test of aboriginal recognition.
After all, aboriginals have enjoyed limited forms of self-rule on
reserves for decades.)

A second variant is that of asymmetrical federalism, something
that would imply rather different treatment of Quebec (and of
aboriginal peoples) than of English Canada. But, in turn, it would
bring significant changes to Quebec and aboriginal input into governance at the central level (and in the case of aboriginals, at the
provincial one, too).

The underlying principle behind asymmetrical federalism is that
of reciprocity. If Quebec, in fact, seeks an array of powers, for
example, over culture, immigration, housing, or social services, that
no other province requires or seeks, why not cede these to Quebec —
but at a price? Quebec would lose the ability to make decisions for
the rest of Canada in all such areas, and would lose any claims to
equalization payments, as well. Quebec parliamentarians and Cabinet ministers in Ottawa would have diminished powers when compared to their analogues from the nine other provinces and two
territories. But the National Assembly and the Government of Quebec would have gained powers. Similarly, albeit on a smaller scale,
aboriginal nations might gain new areas of jurisdiction in territories
that they control. But, in turn, they would lose input into decision-
making in these areas, both provincially and federally, and would
eventually forfeit claims to fiscal transfers for them.

Asymmetrical federalism has both advantages and disadvantages.
It moves the recognition, both of Québécois and of aboriginal
peoples, as distinct nations within Canada a giant step forward. It
gives to each of these the ability to decide just how much autonomy
is required. On the other side, it allows English Canadians to carry
on with the type of federal-provincial arrangements they currently
enjoy. It may even help strengthen the internal cohesion of English
Canada in areas like culture where Quebec (and aboriginal peoples)
opt out. At the same time, it avoids any semblance of allowing
Quebec (or aboriginals) to have their cake and eat it, too, since
autonomy for each comes with a price tag.

The principal disadvantage of asymmetrical federalism, from the

English-Canadian point of view, may be that it acknowledges differences, thereby sundering the notion of a single Canada once and for all. A semblance of unity may be preserved in those areas where Québécois and aboriginals continue to come under federal jurisdiction. But, potentially, we may have set down a slippery slope in which differences will weigh ever larger in the balance. From the Québécois and aboriginal point of view, asymmetrical federalism may be too costly. It opens the door to autonomy, but it closes the tap to fiscal transfers, as well. And it clearly diminishes the Quebec role in Ottawa, possibly fatally. Québécois, particularly of the non-sovereigntist variety, have been very good at playing the federal system to their advantage; one thinks of the role of Quebec caucuses within the governing party in Ottawa in recent decades. Are Quebec politicians, for example, from the Liberal Party, and for that matter the beneficiaries of federal cultural or social policies, prepared to forfeit such advantages under a system of asymmetrical federalism based upon reciprocal gains and losses? There is some room for doubt.

Yet a third variant would take us outside of the current federal system altogether to something closer to a true confederation. Under such a scheme, Quebec would enjoy exclusive control over most areas of current federal jurisdiction, along with those already under provincial control, while aboriginal peoples might acquire wholesale powers within territories under their control. As a result, the current federal government would essentially become a government for English Canada, with a Triple-E Senate probably the price of keeping outer Canada and Ontario, with its half of English Canada's population, in tandem.

The difficult question is less that of the internal governance of English Canada or Quebec (although aboriginal nations might have problems of size, scale, and economic viability in this regard); rather, it is how to bring these different nationalities together within the rubric of a single-state structure. What, in other words, would the confederal level look like and how would it operate given the three-to-one ratio of English Canada's population to Quebec's, not to mention the relatively small number of aboriginal people?

In a book entitled *Toward a Canada–Quebec Union*, I sketched the possible modalities of a confederal union. I would extend the model today to include aboriginal peoples separately. But the areas of jurisdiction that English Canada, Quebec, and aboriginals might want to share would, I think, include foreign policy, defence, trade, currency, citizenship, and quite possibly the environment. We might want a mixture of executive, legislative, and bureaucratic institutions along the lines of what the European Community has developed, with a weighting of representation and influence at this confederal level to reflect the country's demography. It would probably make sense to have a government and Parliament of any Canada–Quebec–aboriginal union made up of delegates from each of the constituent members. Where English Canada, in particular, is concerned, it would be altogether too cumbersome to expect direct election of provincial legislatures, a federal Parliament for English Canada, and representatives to a Canada–Quebec–aboriginal assembly, as well.

A confederal scheme would make sense if Quebec wished to press the case for additional powers along the lines of something like the Allaire Report (that is, 22 areas of jurisdiction transferred from Ottawa). For under such circumstances, English Canadians would not accept Quebec MPs or Cabinet ministers continuing to play a role alongside their English-Canadian counterparts when it came to questions of forming a government or confidence and nonconfidence. It would make far more sense, then, for English Canadians to seek a Parliament and government of their own.

Yet many would see a confederal-type arrangement as a second- or even third-best choice. For certain purposes, especially in the international arena, Canada would still be one. Internally, however, this cohesiveness would translate into an awkward, even cumbersome, joint level of government, with English Canada, Quebec, and the aboriginal nations enjoying maximum autonomy otherwise. There would always be the danger, greater than under asymmetrical federalism, of the entire arrangement falling apart in a moment of crisis. One need only imagine a major difference between English Canada and Quebec on a matter of foreign policy of the type that divided English and French Canadians during the two world wars.

Such possible drawbacks lead us then to a fourth variant: separate nation-state status for each of Canada's nationalities. A sovereign

Quebec would certainly fulfill the dream of many Quebec nationalists, representing a clean break from the rest of Canada. From the
English-Canadian point of view, it might have the advantage of
avoiding the entanglements and conflicts that second- (or third-)
best arrangements entail. And aboriginal peoples who aspire to
international recognition would come into their own.

Yet the problems with nation-state status would be acute. First
and foremost would be that of boundaries. Does Quebec leave
Confederation with its current territory or that of 1912 or 1898 or
1867? What about Quebec claims to parts of Labrador? What about
its aboriginal population, concentrated primarily in northern Quebec? What if they refuse to be part of a sovereign Quebec? Would
we be planting the seeds not only of new Indian wars, but of a
broader Canada–Quebec conflagration?

How would aboriginal governments be structured for international purposes? Scattered in bits and pieces across a half continent,
what sort of connections would they have to one another? Would
they not risk becoming South Africa-style bantustans, dependent on
the goodwill of their much larger and more powerful neighbours?

What sort of economic and other arrangements would be possible
between a sovereign Quebec and English Canada? The division of
the debt, we know already, would be one problem. Others would
include the division of federal assets, the treatment of linguistic
minorities, and trade relations with the United States, not to mention
the need to factor in the resentment, even backlash, that would
accompany a less than amicable separation.

There are thus five scenarios we need to consider in thinking
ahead: the status quo, devolution, asymmetrical federalism, confederal arrangements, and three (or more) sovereign nation-states. Each
of these, other than the status quo, forces English Canadians to
confront difficult questions about their own identity. Each of these,
including the status quo, has its downside where one or both of our
other national communities are concerned.

I am less interested in staking out a particular position here than
in highlighting the options that we face. We need to flesh out middle
options like asymmetrical federalism that have not been clearly
enunciated until now. And we need to be prepared to carry on the

debate when and if the moratorium on constitutional matters that followed Charlottetown is lifted.

This chapter is not a plea for renewed constitutional discussions. It stems from the simple recognition that in the Canadian context such debate may well serve as a surrogate for the type of nonverbal conflicts that have been tearing other multinational federations apart. So thinking English Canada also means rethinking constitutional arrangements. Charlottetown may only have been a station along the way.

11

The Market and the Muse

THE 19TH-CENTURY POLISH POET Adam Mickiewicz, in the opening of *Pan Tadeusz,* addresses his homeland with the words: "You are like health / Only he who has lost it knows what it is." For a Pole living in exile in Paris in the aftermath of the crushing of the 1830 insurrection by the troops of Tsar Nicholas I, the loss of country had a raw and personal quality. It required no flight of fancy to understand what price Poland had paid for the three partitions and for continuing foreign occupation. The poets, intellectuals, and artists would help carry a sense of nation forward into the 20th century and do their part, both during World War II and more recently during the long decades of Soviet domination, to keep the dream of an independent Poland alive.

What applies to Poland pertains to many other national communities around the world. The image of the nation takes shape in words and music, dance and film; symbols such as flags and national anthems take on a power all their own; verses and texts imbibed in school live on long after children have gone their adult ways; a nation's tragedies and triumphs shape later generations in unfathomable ways.

Nations touch the emotions and the passions. They evoke a vision of community, a sense of interrelatedness to others that carries people beyond the sphere of purely private interests or pursuits. They speak to a rootedness in something larger than ourselves — perhaps not quite the *polis* or *res publica* of Classical times — but the closest we seem to have come to re-creating these in modern guise. Nor is nation, as I argued earlier, quite the same thing as state. It is more difficult to stir a sense of identification with what Nietzsche correctly called this cold monster among cold monsters, namely the state, than the loyalties, at times excessive, even blind, that we moderns can and do show to the nation.

One need not refer to the extreme case of war — not uncommon in our 20th century — to recognize the latent chords with which nation and nationalism resonate. Language, culture, history, and collective identity pack tremendous appeal. They become part of the daily lived experience of a people, colouring its outlook and shaping its attitude toward the world outside. One of the enduring lessons of the two centuries since the French Revolution is that national sentiment is no passing phenomenon. Whatever form it may take — fascist, conservative, liberal, socialist, secular, religious, muted, or strong — it has a dynamic of its own.

To no small degree, that dynamic reflects the particular spirit of a people. In the case of the Poles, for example, there has been a romantic side to national aspirations; in the case of the French, a revolutionary; in the case of the Germans, a metaphysical; in the case of many minority peoples around the world, a tragic.

In English Canada, national sentiment has been less prominently displayed than in other societies. This may, in part, have been a reflection of the relatively derivative forms of our political institutions, economic linkages, and cultural values over time. It may, in part, also reflect a deeper English-Canadian disposition.

For the spirit of English-Canadian nationalism has been of a self-doubting, even self-deprecating kind. English-Canadian commentators have made something of a pastime posing the question, "Is there a Canadian identity?" The tendency has been to answer in a conditional tone, as though Canada's survival had to it a permanently provisional character. Many were the English Canadians who had historically voted with their feet by migrating to the United States. Many more put only limited faith in the possibility and, in some cases, even the desirability of Canada surviving as as independent entity in the northern part of North America. Sober realism suggested that, built upon east-west lines, Canada defied both geography and economics. Romantic notions held little sway.

Perhaps one can go so far as to attribute to English Canadians an anti-nationalist sense of nation. By this I mean a certain unease with asserting, in too categorical a fashion, particular characteristics of the English-Canadian mind-set. Other nations might be firmer in their beliefs, hardened or chastened by the conflicts they have been through, but English Canadians, spared life-and-death conflicts through most of their existence, are less prone to take questions of national sentiment so seriously. The culture of English Canada tends to reflect this attitude.

I do not mean to suggest that national sentiments were not present or did not come to the surface, especially in periods of crisis like world war. Even in peacetime, forms of English-Canadian national-ism would emerge, sometimes in relationship to Quebec, more often in relationship to the United States. Yet English Canadians as a people are not given to wearing their patriotism on their sleeves. As a result, English Canada appears in some ways as a nation that dares not speak its name.

To wax lyrical about such a nation is difficult, however often poets may invoke the Canadian Shield, lakes, fauna, or flora. To dramatize the history of a nation so diffident about its own history is also an uphill battle. It is almost as though English Canadians are allergic to that moment of recognition that comes from calling themselves a people, content at most with the symbolic trappings of centenaries or flags rather than with deeper existential commitments. Indeed, it is often the newest Canadians, freshly minted in their allegiance, who bring the greatest passion to this cause.

English Canada's negative national consciousness — its missing national muse — may be rooted in something else, a force that almost as much as geography has shaped the country. My reference is to economic factors and to what, in today's parlance, one is tempted to call the market.

Like the British, Americans, or Dutch, English Canadians have had a strongly commercial vocation. The history of this country, as staple theorists like Harold Innis pointed out long ago, was built on the export of fish, fur, square timber, wheat, and minerals. Banks and financial institutions have deep roots going back to pre-Confederation Canada; public finance for canal and railway building underlay the project to amalgamate the British North American colonies. For our first 50 years as a country, railways and tariffs were the raw stuff of Canadian politics. Depression, Keynesianism, and our repositioning within an American-dominated world economy were the hallmark of the next 50 years. And in the most recent phase, moves to regional trading blocs in Europe, North America, and the Far East, as well as pressures to adopt more market-driven policies across the board, have become the norm.

To a significant degree, the vocabulary of Canadian politics has been economically driven. Sir Allan MacNab, one of the prime ministers of the United Canadas in the 1850s, argued bluntly, "Railways are my politics." The National Policy of 1878–79, possible reciprocity with the United States in 1911, policies for economic recovery in the 1930s and the postwar years, the question of foreign investment in the 1960s, and of free trade in the late 1980s and beyond, are further illustrations of the centrality of economic themes.

At times, this economic preoccupation has led to the use of the state as an instrument of economic development, something that was certainly the case in the late 19th century when protectionism was the norm. It was also the case, until recently, in 20th-century Canada, with crown corporations created, both provincially and federally, for a whole variety of reasons. At a certain level, as authors such as Herschel Hardin have argued, the Canadian entrepreneurial culture was a public enterprise one.

But only at a certain level. Far more characteristic has been the large concentration of private wealth found in all capitalist societies. To a significant degree, for instance, in transportation, merchandising, finance, and certain areas of manufacturing, this concentration was Canadian-based and controlled. But to a striking degree, at least by the standard of other advanced industrial societies, Canada was to experience foreign ownership and control. With it came a feeling of dependence on external powers, coupled with corresponding scepticism about Canada's ability to forge its own destiny in economic matters.

One should also underline the great political power that flows from overweening economic might. In the framing of railway policy in the 1870s or in the selling of the Free Trade Agreement in the

1980s, it is no exaggeration to say that the economic elite dictated the political agenda. At other times, the relationship between corporate and political spheres has been more subtle, as other economic interests, for instance, small business, farmers, or workers, have been able to make their voices heard. Yet in a society like ours, great wealth brings with it privileged access to key governmental ministries and officials and to dominant political parties; control over the principal channels of communication — newspapers, radio, television and cable companies, and publishing houses; and influence over a plethora of nonprofit organizations, including charities, hospital boards, and postsecondary educational institutions. Too often it would appear that what is good for corporate Canada is equated with the good of Canada as a whole. Over the past decade, in particular, there have been concerted attempts by lobby groups such as the Business Council on National Issues or business-financed think tanks like the Conference Board of Canada, the C. D. Howe Institute or, on the extreme right, the Fraser Institute to make us believe so.

That such views find support among significant sectors of English-Canadian society no one can deny. That we will be able to articulate a compelling sense of nation with little more than such economic nostrums is another matter. The marketplace is not the summum bonum of human existence, as philosophers since the Greeks have known. Corporations can be just as destructive as they are supportive of community (or national) interests, something all the more apparent in the age of global capitalism.

We need countervailing values like equality, redistributive justice, and social safety nets to balance out the otherwise predatory values of the market. We need political institutions like government to do some of the reallocation, for example, through a progressive tax system and ideally through taxes on wealth and inheritance, without which the market creates an unacceptable degree of inequality. And we need, deeply implanted within English-Canadian civil society, a sense of community that individuals and associations of all kinds can draw upon and share.

So let us return, once again, to the muses. One of the more interesting, if stillborn, attempts at citizen-based politics in recent years was the Spicer Commission of 1990–91. True, it was manipulative where Brian Mulroney and the federal Conservatives in the aftermath of Meech were concerned. True, it had an amateurish quality to it, both in its proceedings and in its final report. Yet the Citizens' Forum did provide an opportunity for 300,000-odd English Canadians (participation rates in Quebec were dramatically lower) to come together in small groups for several hours at a time and to articulate a view of place and country. From all evidence, and this despite the cynicism of many in the press and politicians in the national parties, those who came forward spoke with a conviction that English Canadians rarely show. There was a concern about the future of Canada that reflected something more than economic self-interest. There was an attempt, however fledgling, to grapple with the reality of Quebec's distinctiveness and aboriginal identities. A hint of im- agination was in the air.

What we may well need in thinking English Canada is something of the same sentiment that surfaced during the public discussions of the early 1990s. Perhaps it is only insistent demands from Quebec, as in the Meech and Charlottetown period, that makes this possible. Perhaps demands from Canada's aboriginal peoples. Perhaps a heightened realization of the dangers that flow from continent-wide economic integration. To rephrase the passage from Mickiewicz with which this chapter began, "It is only when one has lost (or risks losing) one's country that it suddenly looms large."

Ledgers and balance sheets are one thing, deeper currents of national solidarity another. Just how much are ordinary English Canadians prepared to invest in an effort to strengthen and preserve their common bonds within a restructured Canadian federation? Sooner, rather than later, we shall be put to the test. And it is not the gods of commerce who should be our principal guides in the quest, hemming us in with interminable discussions of the national debt or monetary institutions.

English Canada's novelists and filmmakers, songwriters and thes- pians, have their work cut out for them. A little like their counterparts in Quebec in the 1960s, theirs may be the task of articulating a vision of English Canada that touches the wellsprings of identity. Mine is not a call for strident nationalism or grandiloquent declarations. We need, however, to articulate that sense of place and space that makes for a national community, even as we simultaneously come to terms with the increasingly internationalized world we inhabit. "Culture is our politics" is an appropriate credo for the nation we need to invent.

12

A Nation That Dares Not
Speak Its Name

B EFORE CONCLUDING THIS DISCUSSION, let me emphasize one last time just how fraught with diffi-
culty any attempt to "think English Canada" really is. The very term
English Canada is contestable, and speaks to parts of a national psyche
whose sense of identity is caught up with a larger entity called
Canada. If it ever came to a breakdown between Quebec and the rest
of Canada, the inhabitants of the latter would call themselves Canadians, not English Canadians. And any union, confederation, or
association that might accompany such a transformation would be
between Canada — not English Canada — and Quebec.

So the term *English Canada* is something of an ugly duckling that
few wish to embrace. At most, it serves a heuristic purpose, helping
to differentiate the non-Quebec, nonaboriginal parts of Canada. Yet
it risks provoking the ire of various multicultural communities who
may interpret the term as giving privileged status, not only to a
language, but to a founding group. And it risks provoking even
stronger resistance from those who will see it as playing into the hands
of Quebec nationalists, only too eager to win converts in the rest of
Canada to their own Machiavellian schemes. By ceding in the matter
of terminology, so the argument might go, one is ceding the argument in advance.

These criticisms need to be taken seriously, suggesting the need
for close attention to the name we use to designate ourselves. But
they also point to a larger problem that epitomizes the Canadian

predicament. How can we begin to see through the surface differences of our political life or the fault lines that language, culture, or aboriginal versus nonaboriginal identity pose, if the majority group in Canada, by which I mean its largely English-speaking inhabitants, refuse to think of themselves in national terms? It does little good to speak of openness or sensitivity to others or to trumpet a willingness to seek accommodation and compromise, when in their heart of hearts a majority of English Canadians refuse to tackle the underlying question of their own identity. By insisting on their stake in the larger Canadian amalgam, by implying that the Canadian pole must override such lesser identities as Québécois or aboriginal, they are, in fact, seeking to impose their own particular version of nationality. In the process, they are also denying a uniquely English-Canadian dimension to themselves.

There will be no resolution to our crisis as a federation as long as English Canadians refuse to think of themselves as a nation. That is why, in the opening chapter, I sought to distinguish between the concept of nation and that of state. Nation, by my definition, speaks to a sociological sense of self, one coloured by language culture, geography, or history. State, by comparison, speaks to the notion of sovereignty and to the political structures that follow from this.

My argument throughout has been that we need to start thinking of English Canada as a *sociological* nation. This does not mean a politically sovereign English-Canadian state; nor does it mean the end of an ongoing federal or confederal set of arrangements in the northern half of North America. But it does mean recognizing that we live within a multinational federation, and it further means that we, the English Canadians (or the Canadians, in contradistinction to the Québécois and the aboriginal people), have our own raison d'être.

We must stop being a nation that dares not speak its name. Whatever we choose to call ourselves — and I am using English Canada as a shorthand term for the moment — we must get on with the necessary task of sorting things through. The various crises that we have had to confront on the Quebec front since the 1960s, on the aboriginal front more recently, have certainly pushed the process of self-reflection along. The ongoing dilemma of surviving as an

English-speaking society side by side with the United States is another staple of our existence. The fact that we have new challenges to meet like globalization, south-north inequality, or environmental degradation provides a further context for our debates. But debate things we must.

Out of the recent federal election, out of Charlottetown and Meech, out of the 1980 referendum on sovereignty-association, has come a growing perception that Quebec will require a different relationship to what we call Canada than the rest of us. This observation is not a matter of buying into the sovereigntist argument; nor is it a matter of rolling over and allowing Quebec any version of special status its elites may wish to foist on us. There will be hard, tough bargaining accompanying any restructuring of the Canadian federation, with no unilateral concessions made by anyone nor to anyone. For any future constitutional package to receive the sanction of referendum approval, it will need to address the needs and agendas of English Canada, Quebec, and aboriginal people simultaneously.

What then constitutes the English-Canadian agenda? I have tried to explore this in the middle chapters of the book, touching on such topics as language, geography, political culture, regionalism, and multiculturalism. I am the first to recognize the tentative, nay halting, character of the discussion. There is a great deal more that needs to be said about what is constitutive in the use of English as the dominant language of English Canada and about some of the problems that linking language to identity may pose. This dilemma is true not only for new Canadians from linguistic backgrounds other than English, but for second- or fifth-generation English-speaking Canadians trying to stake out a place in the larger English-speaking world.

Politically I am convinced that English Canada must be built on a pluralistic blend of conservatism, liberalism, and social democracy rather than on a hard and unyielding version of any one of these. Canadian political life, at least at the federal level, has had a spirit of give-and-take for much of our history. It would be tragic if something of that same spirit did not characterize things into the future. Polarization of the sort we have sometimes experienced at the provincial level in places like British Columbia is not a propitious model to guide us. We will need to appeal to common citizenship and values in evoking English Canada. We need to bring together elements of tradition and of individual rights, of constitutionalism, parliamentarism, and occasionally direct democracy, of market and of the social net as well.

We will also need to balance off various strands, for example, multiculturalism with the loyalties owed to a shared English-Canadian nationality; region and its tropisms with a territory spanning a continent; group identities, for instance, gender, religious creed, sexual orientation with nongroup specific ones. For no one element can seek to appropriate the concept of English Canada and mark it entirely as its own.

My purpose in setting pen to paper has not been to offer up a definitive version of what English Canada is. My goal has been to help provoke a long overdue discussion of the specifically English-Canadian pole that makes up Canada. While the question of Canadian identity is a perennial one that has preoccupied generation after generation of academics, writers, and political figures, the question of English-Canadian identity is more blurred. It has been caught up with larger discussions about Canada. So much has this been the case that it is often seen as provocative, even gauche, to focus on the specifically English-Canadian component.

We live in the 1990s, however, and it is my contention that what used to be called "the Canadian question" has now become "the English-Canadian question." We need to disaggregate the specific- ally English Canadian from the Canadian *tout court*. We need to stop using Quebec or aboriginal peoples as hostages to our refusal to confront our own identity. We need to give our imaginations freer rein.

Perhaps the call of this book will fall on deaf ears. In a post- Charlottetown, post-election climate, it may be tempting to retreat from public debate as wrenching as that over our identity within a multinational federation like Canada, however much the Bloc Québécois may attempt to stoke the fires. Then there is the economy to keep us on edge: a lingering (or is it chronic?) recession, global restructuring with its accompanying deindustrialization of First

World economies, the crisis of public finance and taxation, the emergence of a new two-class society — those with high-paying jobs and those without. And, of course, there are always environmental calamaties or ethnic conflicts in a post-Cold War world that threatens to be no more harmonious than the one we have just left behind, even if we often choose to blot such news out.

My feeling, nonetheless, is that we can only postpone a debate on the nature of English Canada, not avoid it. An Estates General (or Consultative Assembly) for English Canada may not be for tomorrow. But by 1995 or 1997 it may sound like a remarkably tepid proposal, one whose hour has already passed, as we get on with constitutional restructuring of what remains of the Canadian federation. My own position, for what it is worth, can be summarized in a concluding sentence. By citizenship, I wish to continue to be a Canadian (or the member of a Canadian union of some kind); but by nationality, I am perfectly comfortable to call myself an English Canadian.

The Referendum of October 26, 1992

I N THE AFTERMATH of the third Canada-wide referendum in our history, are there any readers whose eyes do not glaze over at the mere mention of "division of powers," "Senate reform," and the like? Do we really need to revisit the site of our late constitutional battles when there seems close to unanimous agreement to let the corpse of Charlottetown, like Meech before it, rest in peace?

I am no more of a masochist than my fellow citizens, yet there was something as strange about the post-referendum silence that befell the country as about the surfeit of constitutional commissions, committees, and conferences that previously held Canadians in thrall. Most of the political class of this country, federal and provincial, key interest groups from big business to organized labour, editorial writers and media pundits, experts in law, political science, and aboriginal matters, lent their support to the Charlottetown Accord. Yet a majority of francophone Quebeckers, English-speaking Canadians, and status Indians, disdaining the injunctions of their betters, saw fit to vote No. Surely this rare expression of popular sovereignty, however unwelcome it may have proven to the gatekeepers of parliamentary and party legitimacy, merits some attention.

Why, after all, did Canadians not jump at the opportunity to put our constitutional *malheurs* behind us once and for all, as the signatories of Charlottetown had hoped? What strange alliance of opposites led to 56.5 percent of Québécois voting against an agreement that (with one or two exceptions) they saw as giving Quebec too little, and better than 60 percent of western Canadians voting against an agreement that (again with a handful of exceptions) they saw as giving Quebec too much? Was it the spell of Pierre Trudeau, as his enemies in Ottawa and the provincial capitals might suggest, that kept public opinion, especially in English Canada, captive to an outdated vision of a single, unhyphenated Canada? Were the aboriginal self-government provisions a trip wire for rednecks opposed to any ensconcement of aboriginal rights? But, if so, why did status Indians fail to follow the lead of Ovide Mercredi and other aboriginal leaders in endorsing the accord? There seem to be enough unanswered questions to justify a postmortem.

Nonetheless, something more is required than just a blow-by-blow chronology of the two months that separated the signature of the Charlottetown Accord and its demise on the night of October 26. Nor is there much purpose in attempting to score debating points at the expense of proponents of the accord. The author, along with what turned out to be a convincing majority of Canadians and a whopping two-thirds of British Columbians, was on the No side on October 26. Reasons for opposing the accord, however, were as diverse as those for voting in its favour. Independently of any individual's position on the referendum, there is the need to address underlying lessons of the experience.

Let me begin with an observation. The seeds of Charlottetown's failure were already planted in the failure of Meech Lake. In the three years between the ratification of the Meech Lake Accord by Quebec's National Assembly and its expiration on the floors of the Manitoba and Newfoundland legislatures, a sea change occurred in the attitude of a majority of English Canadians toward their elected politicians. They became suspicious of those in office both at the provincial and, a fortiori, at the federal level. Some of this distrust was the result of economic downturn and job loss, coinciding as it did with the introduction of Canada–U.S. free trade in the wake of a divisive and polarizing federal election. Some of it was a reflection of growing anti-Quebec feeling following the invocation of the notwithstanding clause by the Bourassa government in December 1988 (in response to the Supreme Court ruling on Quebec's sign legislation) and passage of Bill 178. And some of it was a reaction, all the more striking because so unexpected, to the top-down style of constitutional deal-making and negotiating that the Meech Lake Accord came to symbolize.

This last feature bears underlining, for it feeds directly into the Charlottetown debate. Throughout most of their history, Canadians have been characterized by a deference to authority. They were prepared to take a back seat on most political questions, allowing their leaders, with their parliamentary/legislative majorities, to act in their name; they did not scrutinize too closely the workings of the party system, allowing a fair degree of internal self-selection and laying on of hands in the designation of candidates; they reelected governments over and over again, both at the provincial and federal levels — one thinks of such figures as Oliver Mowat and L. A. Taschereau, Maurice Duplessis and Joey Smallwood, W. A. C. Bennett and Ernest Manning, John A. Macdonald, Wilfrid Laurier, or William Lyon Mackenzie King. True, from time to time, especially in western Canada or in Quebec, one saw the emergence of new political parties that helped break the mould and challenge establishment ideas. But grass-roots democracy was rapidly channelled and tamed, and populism, more often than not, became the harbinger of new political dynasties. (One thinks of the experience of Social Credit and of the Union Nationale.)

What has been happening in the Canada of the early 1990s is somewhat different. It is not that Canadians have become transformed into Rousseauean citizens, living and breathing the virtues of small-scale democracy and republican good. Nor is it even a matter of wholesale dissatisfaction with existing political parties, despite the emergence of new formations like the Reform Party, the National Party, or the Bloc Québécois. Rather, there is a malaise about the representative character of our political system, its responsiveness to ordinary citizens and their concerns, its ability to help us define our identities and preserve these in a period of geopolitical flux and mercurial economic change.

In truth, the late 20th century has witnessed extraordinary transformations that few can really fathom. From the collapse of communism and the emergence of trading blocs in Europe, East Asia, and North America, from mass starvation in Africa to religious irredentism, from the failures of Keynesianism and of planned command economies to the scourge of monetarism and neoconservatism's unregulated greed, nothing is without its underside. Some of this disillusionment, naturally enough, spills over into a distrust of political processes and elites and has given rise to what, in Europe, has been dubbed a "democratic deficit." The problems the Maastricht Treaty have encountered illustrate this clearly enough. Similarly, in the United States, revulsion with the politics of complacency helped end 12 years of Republican rule.

The defeat of the Charlottetown Accord speaks to something deeper that Meech first helped trigger. We no longer trust our politicians to speak for us in all matters political; indeed, constitutional politics has become a litmus test for much else we find bewildering, even unacceptable, about the direction Canada has been moving in recent years. Before we take the Canadian constitution apart, the better to put it together again, we need to have greater confidence in those who preside over our collective destinies. We need to be surer of just who we are and of what we want to become. We also need to be assured that the process by which constitutional changes are wrought is unambiguously transparent and participatory in a way that constitutional changes of an earlier era were not.

There might be something to be said for a psychological, not to say psychoanalytical, explanation of the intense loathing that Brian Mulroney engendered in English Canada. It is, after all, curious that the electorate, having twice put a political party and its leader into office (albeit with only a minority of the popular vote the second time around), should have turned on a prime minister with such passion. Was it the need to kill the father or, more correctly, the stepfather, whose promises had consistently been broken? Was it disdain for a style of politics, earnest, soothing, yet ultimately facile, that failed to address more profound national longings? Was it the need to find a ritual victim for our own splintered sense of national community, the messenger and his imperfect message becoming the lightning rod of our discontent? A bit of each of these was undoubtedly at work.

This antipathy in turn helps explain the curious adulation that the once-disgraced and retired prince, Pierre Elliott Trudeau, has enjoyed in matters constitutional, both in the Meech debate and in that of Charlottetown. For some, particularly adherents of the Charter of Rights and Freedoms and of an unadulterated version of individual rights, his vision of Canada has become a primordial one with which we can only tamper at our peril. To such supporters, it scarcely matters that there was no charter in place before 1982 or that individual and group rights make uneasy bedfellows in many modern-day polities of the multicultural and multinational sort. For others, the appeal of Trudeau is somewhat different. To them, his vision encompasses a sense of country, nay nation, that seems to transcend regional, linguistic, and ethnic loyalties, conjuring up a view of the federal government as more than just a plaything of the provinces. While the practice of the Trudeau years may not have lived up to the promise, the myth of a single Canada has powerful resonance. Intellectually, moreover, Trudeau had a veritable philosophy when compared to the shallow precepts and practices of his successor.

No wonder, then, that Trudeau's vigorous denunciation of Charlottetown in his *Maclean's* article and then his La Maison Egg Roll speech should have struck such a chord and helped legitimize opposition in quarters that would have found the criticisms of the Reform Party or of the National Action Committee on the Status of Women (NAC) unpersuasive. No wonder also that the provincial premiers should carry relatively little weight with that portion of English-Canadian opinion looking for larger national purpose and principles in a constitution. Perhaps Canadians needed the moral authority of the old lawgiver before they would dare challenge the authority of any would-be new one.

Beyond Trudeau, however, there was the decidedly democratic flavour to public opinion in the post-Meech period. The Spicer Commission Report tapped into this sentiment with its June 1991 findings of widespread mistrust of politicians and support for ideas like constituent assembly. The Beaudoin-Edwards Parliamentary Committee on Procedures for Amending the Constitution of Canada also heard dozens of briefs in the winter and spring of 1991, arguing the case for an elected or appointed constituent assembly more reflective of opinion than prime minister or premiers. With the Allaire and Bélanger-Campeau commissions in Quebec weighing in with calls for a referendum on sovereignty by the fall of 1992, support was also growing for the legitimacy of referenda in constitutional matters in English Canada. Provinces like British Columbia had led the way with legislation along these lines in early 1991.

Alas, there would be very careful control from above of the constitutional process from the summer of 1991 on. Behind closed doors, a task force in the Ministry of Constitutional Affairs worked up a new series of proposals released in September 1991 under the title *Shaping Canada's Future Together*. While there was new reference to ideas like Senate reform and aboriginal self-government, there was also a good deal of continuity with Meech Lake. Distinct society, provincial lists for Supreme Court appointees, limits to federal spending powers were all there, along with enhanced provincial powers in a number of areas. Proposals for enhancing the Canadian economic union could not disguise the fundamentally decentralizing character of the package.

A series of public hearings under the aegis of yet another parliamentary committee, Castonguay-Dobbie rebaptized Beaudoin-Dobbie, could not make up for the fact that the federal proposals had, like Meech, been sprung from above. It was with a series of constitutional conferences held from January to March 1992, with representatives of important interest groups and a number of "ordinary Canadians" in attendance, that an element of genuine participation briefly entered the deliberations. New ideas like asymmetrical federalism and the inherent right to aboriginal self-government were advanced, with serious criticisms also being directed at a Triple-E Senate, the economic union, and the like.

The report of the Beaudoin-Dobbie committee paid only limited attention to these concerns. The recognition of the inherent right to aboriginal self-government was its major concession to grass-roots opinion. For the rest, its conclusions closely echoed those of earlier federal proposals, and became the basis for yet another series of closed-door discussions through the spring and early summer, culminating in the July 7, 1992, agreement among the federal government, nine provinces, two territories, and aboriginal representatives. Once Quebec had come aboard in August 1992, we had the full-blown Charlottetown Accord.

While defenders might make much of the debate and discussion that had preceded Charlottetown, critics were not persuaded that the political class had done all that much listening. The voices of "ordinary citizens" seemed to count for little in the end; log-rolling and the imperative of reaching a deal for substantively more. On democratic grounds, Canadians felt only limited affinity with the text. This time they would not need surrogates like Elijah Harper or Clyde Wells to help them voice their dissent. The referendum would provide them with the golden opportunity for democratic input that the ratification process of Meech Lake did not. No one could dispute the outcome; as for its underlying consequences, one at least was that proprietorship over the constitution of Canada would from now on be clearly vested in the people of this country.

There is a second observation that needs to be made about the failure of Charlottetown. The No's of Quebec and of English-speaking Canada were simply not the same. True, Canadian unity, fragile though it may be, would have been more frayed yet had only Quebec or only British Columbia voted down Charlottetown. The fact that a solid majority of western Canadians, no less than Québécois, was on the negative side, that Ontario and Nova Scotia split pretty well down the middle, represented a quintessentially Canadian form of consensus. The No's had fallen only 13,000 votes short in Ontario of carrying seven of the ten provinces, whose *approval* is normally required to *ratify* most constitutional amendments.

A negative consensus, however, doth not a country make. And Pierre Trudeau notwithstanding, I for one do not interpret the No vote in Quebec as a vote for the constitutional status quo. *Tout au contraire.* Although support for sovereignty and/or sovereignty-association has waxed and waned with the seasons of the moon and with the degree of resentment over English Canada's perceived rejection of Quebec over Meech, one variable has held constant: the desire for increased powers for Quebec. This rallying call unites so-called federalists within the Quebec Liberal Party and nationalists of a more autonomist/sovereigntist persuasion. Proposals prepared by Paul

Gérin-Lajoie for the Quebec Liberal Party in 1967, Claude Ryan's Beige Paper of 1980, and the Allaire and Bélanger-Campeau reports of 1991 are variations on a theme — greater powers for Quebec in a host of areas from culture to social affairs to the economy. Quebec has been demanding recognition as a people or nation, rather than a mere province, within Canada. Whether one dubs this demand special status, asymmetrical federalism, or something closer to sovereignty, it entails significant alteration in Quebec's relationship to Canada.

The reason the Charlottetown Accord failed in Quebec was that it fell short of meeting these demands. Critics could point to the benchmark set by the Quebec Liberal Party at its own congress of March 1991 where the Allaire Report had been passed. Where were the 22 new powers called for in that report? Where was the overriding recognition of Quebec's distinctiveness, tucked away as it was in a broader Canada clause? Where were the gains for Quebec to balance off concessions Robert Bourassa had had to make regarding equal representation of provinces in the Senate or on aboriginal rights? How real were the limits to the federal spending power? At the special Quebec Liberal congress at the end of August 1992 where Charlottetown was ratified, Jean Allaire, Mario Dumont, and the young Liberals expressed their dissent.

The willingness of Robert Bourassa and Gil Rémillard to negotiate a "soft" deal with the rest of Canada after having played hardball for 24 months would now backfire. Damaging leaks from senior civil servants early in the referendum campaign, the so-called Wilhelmy affair, suggesting Bourassa had negotiated with a weak hand, further weakened the Yes side. For a majority of francophone opinion, nationalism was not a mere negotiating ploy. The bloc of Allaire-style nationalists, when added to the 35 to 40 percent of the Quebec electorate who supported a sovereigntist option closer to the Parti Québécois, gave the No side 56.5 percent of the vote on referendum night. (For the record it is worth noting that, as in 1980, close to 90 percent of anglophone and allophone voters in Quebec, some 18 percent of the total electorate, voted Yes.)

Did the No vote add up to a ringing endorsement of Quebec sovereignty? Not necessarily, as polls taken before and after the referendum would show. But did it spell more than a reprieve in a

Canada–Quebec confrontation dating back to the Quiet Revolution? Almost certainly not. Somewhere in the not too distant future — half a year, one year, two years? — the old quarrels will resume with their familiar fury.

What then of the referendum results in English Canada? Four provinces — one, New Brunswick, with a large Acadian minority — voted Yes; five others No. New Canadians in relatively large numbers seem to have voted Yes, along with urban dwellers of the upper middle class; a much larger number of middle- and working-class Canadians and of those living in rural areas voted No.

If one further unpacks the results, geographical factors stand out. There were, on a regional basis, at least four battlegrounds in English Canada — the Atlantic provinces, Ontario, the Prairies, and British Columbia (five, if one includes the territories with their small populations). The intensity of opposition to the accord increased as one moved from east to west. In Atlantic Canada, with its high levels of unemployment, dependency on the federal government, and fear of isolation in the event of Quebec independence, support for a deal that promised constitutional peace was strong. Only in Nova Scotia, the most prosperous of the four provinces in question, did the population, by a small margin, buck the trend.

Ontario, the old workhorse of Confederation, played an important role in the negotiations leading up to Charlottetown, much as it had in Meech. Premier Bob Rae proved a dealmaker regarding Senate reform, a champion of aboriginal rights, and a behind-the-scenes interlocutor of Robert Bourassa. If the package were to carry in English Canada, it would have to carry Ontario by a comfortable margin. In fact, Ontario gave only the feeblest possible approval to the Yes side — 50.1 percent — with much of the province outside Ottawa and Toronto voting No. Ontario's *très petit oui* added up to a modest endorsement of the virtues of compromise. Ontario was prepared to accept some weakening of federal powers — but only just; some recognition of Quebec as a distinct society — but only just; a form of Triple-E Senate — but only just. The head might be in it, but not the heart.

The Prairies would prove a different testing ground for English-Canadian opinion. Here, where wave after wave of immigrant had homesteaded and settled, where aboriginal and Métis and European coexisted, where a sense of unhyphenated Canadianism ran deepest, Charlottetown would prove a difficult sell. The precedent of Meech Lake and Elijah Harper's white feather was there in Manitoba; Sharon Carstairs's stern opposition to the new accord would help stiffen the backbone of others. Saskatchewan was in the midst of an agricultural depression, with little popular enthusiasm for constitutional accords. As for Alberta, home of the Reform Party and of the Triple-E concept, how well would a less than effective Senate sell? Poorly. Nor were there vast reservoirs of sympathy for distinct society, and in more right-wing sections of opinion, for aboriginal self-government.

British Columbia, more surprisingly than the Prairies, proved the strongest single barrier to the accord. The fact that the province, for decades, had enjoyed strong in-migration from other provinces and from abroad made its population especially unhappy with the guarantee in perpetuity to Quebec of 25 percent of all House of Commons seats. Nor was there any greater satisfaction with the extra 18 Commons seats each of Quebec and Ontario stood to secure should Charlottetown pass, when compared to British Columbia's measly four. Nor did distinct society or aboriginal self-government — with much of B.C. territory subject to land claims — enjoy unmitigated support. Underlining British Columbia's rock-bottom opposition to Charlottetown, finally, was something more — a desire to demonstrate that British Columbia was no more to be taken for granted in constitutional matters.

The full implications of English Canada's geographically diffuse No need not detain us further. We may, however, ask ourselves two further questions. What did the English-Canadian vote augur for future attitudes toward Quebec? And what did it spell where aboriginal self-government is concerned?

In Quebec's case, it would appear at first blush that Yes voters in English Canada were far more willing to recognize the province's specificity than those on the No side. Many No voters were voting for the constitutional status quo, for the unhyphenated equality of the provinces, et cetera. Only a minority could be said to support the position of NAC or some hypothetical three-nation model of Canada.

If one scratches beneath the surface, however, the majority No in English Canada leaves some hope for renewed dialogue in the future. Special status, defined as increased powers for Quebec that no other province will acquire, is a nonstarter, at least within our *existing* federal framework. But increased powers for Quebec, compensated by a *net decline* in Quebec's power in Ottawa, may yet prove another matter. There has been little discussion of such trade-offs until now.

How many English Canadians, westerners included, would deny the specificity of Quebec where language or culture are concerned? Very few. And how would such English Canadians be likely to react to demands from Quebec for increased powers if the National Assembly and government of Quebec were prepared to pay the price in hard political terms? Potentially more favourably than in the recent past when Quebec politicians, both in Quebec City and Ottawa, have been seen as seeking unilateral advantages for Quebec at the expense of the rest of Canada.

Asymmetrical federalism might mean something as follows. Quebec would indeed acquire exclusive jurisdiction in any number of the areas the Allaire Report listed, for example, communications, culture, housing, labour market training, unemployment insurance, and the province would receive some tax points to help with the fiscal costs that go with such transfers. But, in exchange, Quebec MPs, senators, and Cabinet ministers in Ottawa would have no further say where decision-making in such areas for the rest of Canada were concerned. They would not be able to vote on legislation or participate in parliamentary or Cabinet discussions where such matters were on the agenda. Nor would Quebec be eligible for equalization payments of any kind in areas in which it had opted out.

In practice, such a scheme would lead to significant differentiation of the English-Canadian from the Quebec agenda. Certain days of the week, Parliament or Cabinet would meet without Quebec members present; for certain purposes, the federal government would become the government of English Canada; and in these areas the government would require majority approval from the English-Canadian parliamentarians.

I am not suggesting that asymmetrical federalism of this sort would come without its problems. For example, what would happen if a party/government has majority support within English Canada, but only minority support in Canada including Quebec? Or conversely? At which level would confidence votes make or break governments? Is there not some limit to how many new powers Quebec might acquire and still remain part of an ongoing federal system? How much or how little of official bilingualism would be retained at the federal level in areas where Quebec had chosen to exercise exclusive jurisdiction? All this and more requires extensive debate.

Still, the climate for such discussion promises to be quite unlike Meech or Charlottetown if we are not working to artificial deadlines and if it is clear that Quebec is prepared to give up power for every new power it attains. As long as Quebec public opinion and politicians are up front in recognizing this principle, there is a real possibility of a breakthrough in the rest of Canada. If there is even a hint of Quebec wanting to have its cake and eat it, too, the hostility of English-Canadian opinion to asymmetrical federalism or any equivalent arrangement will prove insurmountable.

Aboriginal self-government is a slightly different proposition. At one level, there seemed to be an unprecedented degree of openness in mainstream opinion to aboriginal concerns during the post-Meech period. There was recognition that First Nations people, by and large, have been excluded from many of the economic and social benefits of Canadian society, that their cultural specificity had been overridden by European-derived values. This new consciousness translated into support for forms of aboriginal self-government, involving considerable autonomy from both provincial and federal governments.

That not everyone supported a "third level" was obvious in the round of discussions culminating in Charlottetown, namely, the reservations of Premiers Wells and Bourassa. The seemingly collectivist and/or ethnic notions of rights contained in Charlottetown attracted the ire of opponents as diverse as the Native Women's Association of Canada and Pierre Trudeau. To these opponents one might add Quebec nationalists and Reform Party supporters, especially nonaboriginals in resource sectors of the country, for example, coastal and interior British Columbia. Finally many status Indians who voted against Charlottetown were concerned about possible benefits and rights that aboriginal people stood to lose.

Aboriginal issues are not about to go away. Indeed, there is a Royal Commission on Aboriginal People slated to report within the next year or two, and an ongoing process of land claims negotiations under way in various provinces. What is going to be required in constitutional matters is balanced discussion of possible trade-offs between increased political and economic powers for aboriginal people, on the one hand, and ongoing claims by aboriginals on nonaboriginal governments and institutions, on the other. There is also the thorny question to be tackled as to whether aboriginal self-government is, in fact, opening the door to sovereignty in the full juridical sense or not. The future response of nonaboriginal Canadians (and Québécois) to aboriginal demands will have a lot to do with how such questions are answered.

The failure of Charlottetown, whatever some may earnestly have hoped, has not put our constitutional travails behind us. For the underlying divisions that preoccupied us so much in recent years, especially those involving Quebec, aboriginals, and the rest of Canada, have not been put to rest. Competing national visions need to be addressed, as does the need for more democratic models of constitution-making and for alternative institutional arrangements. At the heart of any such enterprise will lie the need for a radical rethinking of identities, no more so than in the rest of Canada, that is, English-speaking Canada. This question of identity has been the major theme of a book in which the 1992 referendum, once a point of departure, has become a postscript.